The Brain of the Highly Sensitive Person

Esther Bergsma

THE BRAIN OF THE HIGHLY SENSITIVE PERSON

Why you shouldn't judge a fish by its ability to climb a tree

b:k light

ISBN: 978 94 92595 300

Translation: Vertaalbureau Textwerk B.V.
Design: Andries Mol, Studio Mol
Illustrations: Henk-Jan Panneman Graphic Design

This book was originally published as *Het hoogsensitieve brein*
(2019, ISBN 978 94 92595 12 6, Booklight uitgeverij, The Netherlands)

b:k light

Reviews

Thank you Esther for your commitment and for all that went into this book. I believe you will change a lot of lives! As a psychotherapist and founder of Sensitive Empowerment, I have specialized in the trait of high sensitivity for years and found that learning information about the trait and understanding our brain differences are life-changing. To have research like this is invaluable. I have been a supporter of Esther's research for a long time, even having her as a guest in my Sensitive Empowerment Community where we all participated in support of more research so I am very excited to see this book available and share it with my community! It's incredibly validating to see research and this book will likely become important for years to come. When we understand ourselves we can support ourselves. I love what she shares and totally agree: "Better insight into the functioning of the highly sensitive brain makes the talents of highly sensitive people more visible." That is how we begin to highlight the many gifts of this trait and help HSPs know their incredible value in the world.
Julie Bjelland, LMFT, founder of Sensitive Empowerment

Esther Bergsma's book, *The Brain Of The Highly Sensitive Person*, belongs on the bookshelf of every sensitive person. Esther lays out all the research on the brain and the highly sensitive person and then offers fresh insights on how the sensitive brain works, the pause-and-check system, and the optimal-option-ambition to illuminate how sensitive people function in the world. Esther offers her own experiences to illuminate the insights she offers so sensitive people who want to get a handle on working effectively with their sensitivity understand how to do so. A must read!
Maria Hill, founder of Sensitive Evolution, the Emerging Sensitive Program, and author of The Emerging Sensitive: A Guide For finding Your Place In The World.

The Brain of the Highly Sensitive Person by Esther Bergsma is a thoroughly investigated piece of work and a true page turner. The author succeeds in translating complicated scientific information – the functioning of the highly sensitive brain – into a language that is easy to read and to understand; at the end of each paragraph I felt eager to continue straight into the next one.
This book, based on personal experience as well as the study of much of the available scientific research, is a must read for those who want to know about the workings of the highly sensitive brain, resulting in different ways of thinking, feeling and re-acting.
Karina Zegers de Beijl, consultant on high sensitivity (ICHS, ICF), author

One in five people are highly sensitive. If you have met more than five people in your life, you should read this book. This book brings the hidden talents of your colleagues, friends and children to light. You'll learn why things which seem easy for you are difficult for them, and strategies to help them thrive. And if you are highly sensitive, you'll

recognize yourself in these pages, and learn about how you can be at your best. Esther provides the most accessible explanation I've read of the neuroscience and genetics of high sensitivity, skillfully brought to life with stories and experiences from HSPs.
Rosie Raleigh, founder and CEO of Vantage: Campaigning for equality for highly sensitive people

I have been waiting for this book, more specifically to have a thorough yet accessible assessment of how the highly sensitive brain functions. So many highly sensitive people have similar experiences, as Esther shares through her qualitative research and personal anecdotes throughout the book, but have no explanation of why that experience exists. Using data, illustrations, diagrams, and real-life examples, Esther clearly explains how the highly sensitive brain differs and the talents that result from those differences. This is not only validating but an important reminder of how essential HSP talents are for the survival of our species. *The Brain of the Highly Sensitive Person* is the right balance of relatable and educational, a must-read for every therapist and medical professional.
April Snow, psychotherapist, HSP specialist, author

Esther does a wonderful job synthesizing the latest research on how the highly sensitive person's brain works differently than non-HSPs. Her practical examples from decision making of an HSP at work to how HSP children respond to events illustrate these differences and nuances. If you enjoy in-depth research on the brain, want to understand how HSPs are wired differently and share this knowledge with others, then this book is for you.
Nicole Burgess, Licensed Marriage and Family Therapist and Leadership Coach to highly sensitive professional women.

This is the perfect book for everyone who wants to understand the functioning of the highly sensitive brain. You get the scientific information and illustrations told in a simple and understandable way. Esther Bergsma gives us an understanding of how highly sensitive people are different from non-highly sensitive people and how the highly sensitive brain works in a unique way.
Lian Kirksæther, Norway, ICF-DNCF coach, mentor, ICHS-International Consulants on High Sensitivity, author and trainer specialized on women and high sensitivity

This book is an excellent resource for anyone who wants to understand the brain of the highly sensitive person. Drs. Bergsma has done a beautiful job combining science, research, and anecdotal vignettes to provide a comprehensive and readable guide that anyone can understand. The format is clear, comprehensive and easy to understand. The world needs highly sensitive people (HSPs), and Drs. Bergsma clearly demonstrates the strengths and gifts of HSPs.
Patricia Young, LCSW, therapist, coach and creator of the podcast Unapologetically Sensitive, a podcast for the Highly Sensitive Person.

This book is a great resource for HSPs wanting to understand how their brain and body work as a HSP. The more we learn about what we need as a HSP, the better we can adjust our own environment to meet these needs, helping you to identify your own HSP strengths.
Fiona Stevenson, Holistic Counsellor - Psychotherapist

Table of contents

Introduction

Everybody is a genius. But if you judge a fish by its ability to climb a tree, it will live its whole life believing that it is stupid.
Albert Einstein

I failed. That was all I could think of. Fallen through, fallen short, failed in capital letters. Eight months after I first called in sick, and after an extensive reintegration process, I had called in completely sick again. Things didn't go well. Except worrying, that went very well. My head was constantly making lists. Everything I had not done well in my job as a manager. That time when I should have been decisive or should have exercised my authority. That time I should have enforced the rules strictly. Should have made my opinion quite clear. That time I didn't make a decision fast enough or let myself get stampeded. My brain was constantly producing images of my failure.

It was during that time that I first read a book by Elaine Aron. Although it was difficult to concentrate, this book held my attention. I read about myself in a language I wasn't used to, but recognized nonetheless. I kept rereading this sentence: 'We are designed to think carefully before acting, so we are rarely wrong [...]. We are designed to notice the nuances in a situation and weigh them carefully.'[1]

This new language gave me a different perspective. The images of my failure that my brain so willingly produced were given a different color. Indeed, I had not made a quick decision that one time. But this had helped me identify a major problem, which I could then prevent. Indeed, I was not a manager who strictly enforced rules, but this enabled me to really connect with an employee who had felt trapped under the previous manager for years.
I got to know myself again. Slowly, my brain produced different images about my functioning. And a different self-image emerged. Instead of 'I failed', it became 'I am highly sensitive.' A quality with advantages and disadvantages. Eager to learn, as I am, I wanted to find out as much as possible about this trait. But I soon ran into a few problems.

The care providers I consulted to recover from my burnout were barely familiar with high sensitivity. Sometimes they misinterpreted the trait. For example, elements of the trait were misinterpreted as core ('high sensitivity is sensitivity to sounds'), they equated the trait with related aspects ('high sensitivity is spiritual ability') or with effects of the trait ('high sensitivity is overstimulation'). So I started looking for information at the fundamental level: scientific articles. And because so little was known, I launched a number of quantitative studies myself. Every piece of the puzzle gave a little more insight into the bigger picture.
The picture is not yet complete. Much more research on high sensitivity is needed. But the picture is clearer than most people are aware of. Some misunderstandings are still rampant, even though enough information already exists to refute them. That's why I find it crucial to make that scientific information accessible.

The emphasis in this book is on the functioning of the highly sensitive brain. To understand how highly sensitive people differ from non-highly sensitive people, knowledge regarding the neurological differences is important. These differences explain why highly sensitive people sometimes experience a situation very differently from non-highly sensitive people, or why something has a completely different impact on them. By choosing this angle, I've left some aspects unexplained. I am aware of this. But I believe that this approach can give us new insights into high sensitivity. And that is necessary. The lack of knowledge regarding high sensitivity has consequences for both the individual and our society. We do not only misinterpret people's issues, but also their talents, because we look at them from one specific perspective.

First of all, talents may be wasted. Albert Einstein's quote reflects this nicely. If we judge a fish by its ability to climb a tree, it will live its whole life believing that it is stupid.

We still do not recognize the talents of highly sensitive people enough. On the one hand, because we know little about the highly sensitive brain and the talents it entails. On the other hand, because our society prefers specific talents. In her book *Quiet,* Susan Cain wrote that extroverted talents such as quick decision making, spontaneous action or making easy conversation are highly valued in many Western societies.[2] In families, groups, teams, departments, and relationships this ideal image predominates, and other talents remain unseen.

I like to imagine things in a narrative and imagine that a group of animals has the task of exploring an archipelago. The leader of the team likes to climb trees and knows that this gives him a quick overview of the island and the surrounding waters. He urges his team members to do the same. This way the assignment will be completed quickly. However, to his frustration, not every team member can climb. The non-climbers are therefore given the task of providing food. Including the fish. It provides a large amount of food and both the leader and the fish are satisfied.

At one point, an animal decides that a tree trunk can serve as a bridge to get to the next island. The fish provides helpful clues from his point of view. However, no one considers that the fish can swim around the islands and, in that way, can provide a great deal of valuable information. His real talent isn't utilized.

Secondly, insufficient knowledge of high sensitivity can lead to incorrect interpretations of issues. When a fish complains of a choking sensation and accelerated breathing, a land animal may conclude that the fish has run too fast. He himself experiences these issues when he has run too fast or too long. It does not occur to him that a fish cannot run fast. And he does not consider gill flukes at all, because he is unfamiliar with them himself. Highly sensitive people run this risk of misinterpretation when they talk about their issues.
In her book *Hoogsensitiviteit professioneel gezien* (High sensitivity, professionally speaking), Annek Tol describes that there is a large overlap between issues highly sensitive people experience and symptoms of disorders such as depression, panic disorder, autism spectrum disorder (ASD), ADHD, borderline and chronic fatigue syndrome[3]. If doctors only take these issues into account, an incorrect diagnosis is lurking. Tol illustrates that when people learn to deal with their high sensitivity, a large portion of the issues disappear. This shows that often, it does not entail a disorder, but a temporary inability.
A one-sided framework can therefore lead to incorrect diagnosis. This problem could be bigger than we think. In her book *Psychotherapy and the highly sensitive person,* Elaine Aron writes that although only 20% of people are highly sensitive, probably half of those seeking psychological help are highly sensitive.[4] Highly sensitive people are thus strongly overrepresented in this group. For this reason, knowledge of high sensitivity is indispensable in determining the need for help by professionals.

Thirdly, incorrectly interpreted issues can generate high costs. An incorrect diagnosis in highly sensitive people can lead to inadequate help. Resulting in high costs and years of taking pills, treatments, and therapies that do not contribute to the solution of the actual problem. Moreover, it leads to unnecessarily long absenteeism, with the associated high social costs.[5]
Suppose the fish himself knew that its choking sensation and rapid breathing indicate gill flukes. And perhaps it also knows that water

quality is essential in order to get better. This may be difficult to believe for his parent, teacher, manager, or partner due to different experiences. If he experiences a choking sensation and accelerated breathing, it is because he has run too fast and needs to catch his breath. Take a deep breath of air. He cannot imagine that the problem lies in the water quality. The water looks fine to him. He certainly doesn't want to spend money on this. And so the problem persists.

What does this unawareness mean for a highly sensitive person? He may conclude that he does not see it properly and may try to adapt to the viewpoint and advice of the other. Or come to the conclusion that he, apparently, is 'not normal'. In the coming chapters, I will illustrate that this has an effect on the brain and can increase problems.
If the highly sensitive person remains convinced of his own analysis, then it depends on the willingness of the other, how much energy it takes to make the necessary adjustments. Does he have to challenge everything or is the other willing to seek joint solutions? Hence, both his own conclusions and the reaction of the other are vital.

As long as we do not recognize that there are differences between highly sensitive and non-highly sensitive people, we are missing out on opportunities. Individual talents remain untapped. Issues are not resolved. Moreover, as a social group we miss opportunities because we need the talents of highly sensitive people.

This book is for anyone who wants to learn to recognize highly sensitive talent better. Highly sensitive people, who, like me, have often had negative thoughts about their personality for years and would like to change this. Care providers who want to learn to better interpret people's behavior and/or issues in order to tailor their guidance accordingly. But also (HR) managers who want to use the talents of their highly sensitive employees more effectively.

Reading guide

In chapter 1, I discuss the definition of high sensitivity and how it came about. In chapter 2, the daily life of highly sensitive adults and children is addressed. Many highly sensitive people experience overstimulation, fear of failure or have low self-esteem. As a result, their talents fail to reach their full potential.

The third chapter provides a brief introduction to the brain. I will discuss the most important areas of the brain to make what is known about the highly sensitive brain more comprehensible. At the back of this book a keyword list can be found where all technical terms are explained once more.

In order to structure all research results, I have visualized the functioning of the highly sensitive brain. In chapter 4, I briefly outline the main elements I distinguish, in order to clarify these one by one in the following chapters. The matter of perception is discussed in chapter 5. Chapter 6 focuses on the pause-and-check-system. This is the tendency of highly sensitive people to take the time to process incoming information. In chapter 7, I discuss the optimal-option-ambition. Here, I show that taking into account the social context is ingrained in the highly sensitive brain. Chapter 8 deals with the more intense reaction highly sensitive people have after processing information. They experience more stress, have more intense emotions and the impact of a situation is greater.

Chapter 9 takes a closer look at the stress system and the reason why the highly sensitive brain is more sensitive to stress. Chapter 10 deals with social stress and rejection. Stress and sensitivity to rejection perpetuate each other. In order to get out of that vicious cycle, it is important to make real connections.

Chapter 11 summarizes all the talents of highly sensitive people and demonstrates that you should not judge a fish by its ability to climb a tree.

CHAPTER 1

High Sensitivity

'High sensitivity? That was made up by some marketing genius,' was the reaction I received from my counselor when I cautiously suggested my high sensitivity played a role in the persistence of my issues. I had been ill for a year and a half and showed little improvement. I was still very tired. Every day activities cost me a lot of energy. If I had to do laundry, I would schedule an entire morning for the chore. My mind no longer understood how to distinguish dark from light laundry and, at the same time, pay attention to the washing temperature. Solving that complex puzzle would leave me exhausted. The rest of the morning I would lay on the couch, feeling drained.

At the end of the day – when the kids were in bed – I was glad I could go to sleep myself. But the next morning I would wake up feeling exhausted, again and again, even after nine hours of sleep. I was desperate. How could I get out of this dark place? The many therapists who thought they could help me, failed to do so.

I had always been an exemplary patient: listened carefully to advice, did what they recommended and practiced with full commitment. However, more and more, I had the feeling we were on the wrong track. I had already read a thing or two about high sensitivity and sensed this quality played a role here. I gathered all my courage and raised this issue with my counselor. But as soon as I brought it up, it was abruptly dismissed. High sensitivity was considered a mere fairytale. That hurt. I felt rejected as a person. At the time however, I did not have the energy or the knowledge to change this counselor's mind. I stopped going to that counselor shortly afterwards.

This happened over ten years ago. At that time, knowledge about high sensitivity was not yet widely known. However, to this day, I hear similar stories from other highly sensitive people. This brings me to the basics. What is high sensitivity? And how has its definition come about.

1.1 ELAINE ARON

The general image that exists of highly sensitive people does not quite match what the trait actually entails. In short, highly sensitive people perceive subtle information from their environment and process it in depth. They often need more time to respond to a situation. Therefore, others sometimes perceive highly sensitive people to be inhibited or shy.

In addition, the intense processing of information evokes intense emotions. A highly sensitive person can be upset by relatively small things. As a result, others sometimes find highly sensitive people to be hypersensitive or too emotional.

Moreover, this depth of processing requires a lot of energy, which means that highly sensitive people need a lot of recovery time. This sometimes creates the impression that highly sensitive people cannot cope with much and are always tired.

The terms 'inhibited', 'shy', 'hypersensitive' and 'always tired', however, do not describe the essence of high sensitivity.

American psychological researcher Dr. Elaine Aron was the first to study the quality of high sensitivity. In the early 90s, she launched a research project into sensitivity. Aron was initially interested in the sensitive side of introversion. However, she considered the terminology commonly used – 'shyness' or 'inhibition' – to be incorrect. She appealed to people in the vicinity of Santa Cruz (where she was posted at the university at the time) to sign up for an interview. The number of applications was overwhelming. Eventually, she interviewed 39 people for approximately two hours each.

Through these interviews, she discovered that the sensitive side of introversion is a separate independent trait, distinct from introversion. Some of the people she interviewed actually turned out to be outgoing. Together with her husband, Art Aron, she discussed the results in a scientific article – she as a psychologist and he as a researcher in the field of love[1]. In that particular article, Aron and Aron introduced the concept of sensory-processing sensitivity (SPS). This became the scientific name for what has become known to the public as high sensitivity. In the same period, Elaine Aron wrote the book *The highly sensitive person*, from which the worldwide abbreviation HSP (highly sensitive person) arose.[2]

In that first article, the Aron couple described what high sensitivity entails and how it can be measured. They introduced the so-called HSP scale, a questionnaire with 27 items that measures whether someone is highly sensitive or not. For example: 'I am aware of subtle signals in my environment', 'I am influenced by the mood of others', 'I have a rich and complex inner world', 'I feel rushed when I have to do many things in a short period of time' or 'I am deeply moved by art or music'.

Their first study with the HSP scale showed that introversion and high sensitivity can indeed be clearly distinguished from each other. HSPs are more often introverted than non-highly sensitive people, but one third of HSPs are extroverted.[3] The same was true for the trait emotionality. In personality research, emotionality means that someone experiences many negative emotions. Aron and Aron showed that HSPs more frequently score high on this, but not always. HSPs who have had a good childhood scored even lower on emotionality. They conclude that high sensitivity is a clearly distinguishable trait.

People from all over the world recognize themselves in Elaine Aron's book – 1 million copies have now been sold and it has been translated into 17 languages – but scientists remained critical for a long time. Together with colleagues, Aron has continued to publish scientific articles on high sensitivity, and other scientists have also researched the phenomenon in the past ten years. As a result, more and more information has become available about what distinguishes the high sensitivity trait from other traits.

1.2 NEW SITUATIONS

At daycare centers, it is clearly visible. Children react differently to new situations, even in infancy. When there are new toys in the group or a different care provider comes in, one child reacts differently than the other. One child starts to cry, another immediately engages in the situation, while another watches from a distance until the commotion is over. These innate differences have been widely studied by scientists, each from their own point of view. The observed differences were given various names.

One explanation for the differences between children is the trait of high sensitivity. Some people need more time to process all the information they perceive and therefore react more in a more reserved manner or with a more wait-and-see type of attitude. This intense processing of information – depth of processing – is the central part of high sensitivity.[4] Highly sensitive people think before they act. In an unfamiliar situation, highly sensitive people tread carefully.

Responsivity

Differences in response have also been detected among animal species. Max Wolf and colleagues (2008) have compared studies among more than a hundred animal species and looked at differences in response to new situations, such as deposited food or objects.[5] Wolf concludes that two reaction patterns can be distinguished in all those animal species.

1. A group that reacts impulsively independent of the environment. They often go directly to the food or object. They do not attune to their environment and are therefore called non-responsive.
2. The other group adapts its strategy to the situation and observes (for a while) before taking action. He calls this the responsive group.

The reaction of the second group is very similar to what Aron writes about highly sensitive people. These animals sit quietly or swim exploratory laps first – similar to how highly sensitive people take the time to process information – while other counterparts bravely engage in the new situation. At first glance, this responsive strategy does not seem efficient: waiting hardly helps when collecting food. Moreover, due to the continuous alertness which characterizes this strategy, it costs a lot of energy. This raises the question: why is this group represented in every animal species?

These animals operate more carefully and thus increase their chances of survival in the event of threat. For the survival of the animal species, it is useful that a part of them adopts this prudent strategy. A small part. If the 'cautious' group is too large, new situations are not explored enough and that has negative implications for the survival of the species. The study by Wolf et al. shows that 20% is ideal. This distribution appears to exist in a large number of animal species and mathematical calculations also indicate this as the best option. A small group of responsive animals is thus important for the survival of the species. Coincidence or not, 20% of the world's population is highly sensitive.[6]

Various scientists have independently studied differences between children in different situations (see box). They use various terms to describe the behavior, but they all signal that some children are much more influenced by their environment than others. This is also an important aspect of high sensitivity.

Differences between children in new situations
Jerome Kagan examined the response of four-month-old babies to a colorful mobile. He observed that some children were very relaxed when introduced to this strange object. At toddler age, these children turned out to be easy going. He called them uninhibited. Another group of children kicked their legs, waved their arms and quickly started to cry. Tests showed that this 20% group had a higher stress response. At toddler age, he characterized these children as shy. He called them inhibited.[7]

Thomas Boyce and Bruce Ellis (2005) examined studies of children's stress responses and came to a surprising insight. Some children are hardly affected by the circumstances in which they find themselves. They call them the dandelion children: they always grow, whether on the side of the road or in the cracks of the pavement. For another group of children (which accounted for 20% of the total) the circumstances need to be just right. They need the right amount of light, water, soil and nutrition. Boyce and Ellis call them the orchid children. In a bad situation, these children will not flourish, but when the conditions are perfect, they will flourish. Their theory is called biological sensitivity to context (BSC). In January 2019, *The orchid and the dandelion* was published, in which Boyce makes his findings accessible to the public.

Jay Belsky (2005) also saw this difference. Some children are more sensitive to the way they are raised than others. One group of children experiences little effect from a bad childhood. They also continue to function well during negative life events, such as the death of a parent, a move or in case of neglect. The other group of children does experience problems with a similar bad childhood. They develop health problems or no longer function well at school. However, the same group appears to perform very well if the circumstances are positive – if parents are supportive, for example, or if the learning environment is good – while the first group is barely influenced by this either. They benefit very little from this. Together with Michael Pluess, he called this differential susceptibility (DS): the degree to which you are influenced by your environment.[8]

Pluess, Aron and colleagues (2017) conclude that biological sensitivity to context and differential susceptibility describe the same processes as sensory-processing sensitivity, or high sensitivity. These three concepts describe the reactivity to the environment: one group is hardly influenced by the environment, while the second group is strongly influenced, both in a negative and positive way. Pluess suggests using environmental sensitivity as an umbrella term.

For clarity, I use the term high sensitivity in this book. I use it as a synonym for all theories stated above.

1.3 DEFINITION

Thus, highly sensitive people react in a more reserved manner to new situations and are strongly influenced by their environment. This is caused by the way they process information. They perceive the small things that go unnoticed by others and consider these deeply. Aron sees high sensitivity as 'an innate tendency to pause-to-check in novel situations, greater sensitivity to subtle stimuli, and the engagement of deeper cognitive processing strategies for employing coping actions, all of which is driven by heightened emotional reactivity, both positive and negative.'[9]

What is striking about the definition is that **perceiving, processing** as well as **reacting** to stimuli takes a different course in highly sensitive people. I will explain the three stages of information processing below.

First of all, highly sensitive people notice more. Their nervous system is more sensitive and they are able to perceive subtle stimuli. As a result, highly sensitive people perceive sounds, lights or smells more quickly. This also involves noticing the emotions of others, social interactions and changes made in a certain space.

Secondly, the stimuli are processed in depth. Highly sensitive people do not take action until they have processed the relevant information. They have a so-called pause-to-check system. Aron does not mention what this more intense and complex processing entails. Studies into the functioning of the highly sensitive brain show that HSPs are strongly focused on the social group.[10] I have called this the optimal-option-ambition: the action that best serves the group is preferred. HSPs are strongly focused on the interests of the group and often subordinate their own interests.

Finally, they respond differently to all those stimuli. It takes more energy to better notice all stimuli and process these more deeply, often causing HSPs to experience more stress. In addition, they react more emotionally. Highly sensitive people are strongly influenced by what they perceive, both in situations that evoke negative emotions such as sadness and fear, and in situations that evoke positive emotions.

Aron's definition also mentions the **advantage** of this way of processing information: it leads to more effective action. The energy it takes to better notice and more deeply process all stimuli thus yields added value in effectiveness.

For the description of the highly sensitive brain I took the three stages of information processing as a guideline: perceiving, processing and reacting. I describe how the highly sensitive brain distinguishes itself from the non-highly sensitive brain in this regard. Based on the elements presented above, I use the following definition of high sensitivity in this book:
High sensitivity is a trait characterized by a great sensitivity to stimuli (both internal and external and both positive and negative) and the profound processing thereof. This deep processing process involves both time (the pause-to-check system) and content (the optimal-option-ambition). The greater sensitivity to stimuli in combination with depth of processing leads to a more intense reaction in terms of emotion and/or stress.

1.4 HIGH SENSITIVITY GENE

It is likely that high sensitivity is innate. Studies by developmental psychologists show that differences between children exist from infancy and biological research among a variety of animal species also illustrates congenital differences.

Which gene or – more reasonably – which genes are associated with high sensitivity is difficult to determine. Genes do not determine everything. The extent to which a personality trait is expressed can be influenced by the environment. Within the nature-nurture discussion, reference is now made to the 'gene-environment interaction' (GXE). This means that some genes are only expressed in a certain environment. For example, a lot of adversity in your life can trigger certain traits that would not have emerged if you had only known prosperity. A person's personality will therefore always be a mix of different genes in combination with the environment.

5-HTTLPR

Several studies have shown that the gene 5-HTTLPR influences environmental sensitivity.[11] This gene plays a role in the transport of serotonin. Serotonin is a neurotransmitter: a substance that enables neurons to communicate with each other. Serotonin affects memory, self-confidence, sleep, emotions, sexual activity, appetite, cognition (such as learning, attention, planning) and social behavior. In addition, when the serotonin level is too low, pain stimuli cannot be processed properly.

The 5-HTTLPR gene is polymorphic, which means it has several variants. In this case, a short variant (s allele) and a long variant (l allele). Since every human being has two of these genes, you can have one of three variations: s/s, s/l or l/l. The l allele provides approximately twice the reuptake of serotonin than the s allele. Meaning that serotonin is recycled better and that its concentration can be better regulated if you have the long variety. If you have two s alleles (s/s), the serotonin in your brain is absorbed less well.[12] Which variant you have can therefore have an effect on your emotions, sleep, appetite, and so on.

In his book *Genetics of psychological well-being* (2015), Michael Pluess summarizes, among other things, the research into this gene. For a long time, the focus has been on the resilience of people with an l allele: they are hardly influenced by bad circumstances, while people with one or more s alleles have a greater risk of depression after negative life events. However, newer research shows that an s allele also offers benefits. People with this variant benefit more from positive circumstances. They respond more strongly to their environment, as Pluess concludes: a negative environment leads to issues, while a positive, supportive situation allows them to flourish. Boyce and Ellis' metaphor of the orchid and the dandelion fits perfectly with this (see box). The gene 5-HTTLPR is therefore seen as an indicator of the degree of environmental sensitivity.

Cecile Licht and colleagues (2011) showed an association between high sensitivity and the s/s variant of 5-HTTLPR.[13] Highly sensitive people more often have this variant, also when corrected for gender, age, issues, and other character traits. This means the connection is not influenced by a different characteristic; there is a direct link between high sensitivity and the gene. Together with her colleagues, Judith Homberg from Radboud University Nijmegen shows that there are striking similarities between characteristics of highly sensitive people and characteristics of people with the s/s variant of 5 -HTTLPR.[14] Based on these studies, we can assume that highly sensitive people are more likely to have the s/s genotype.

DRD4 7-repeat

Sarah Moore and Richard Depue (2016) took a broader view. They studied the connection between environmental sensitivity and different neurotransmitters. In their article, environmental sensitivity is used as an umbrella term for biological sensitivity to context, differential susceptibility and SPS (as did Michael Pluess). Moore and Depue examine the connection between environmental sensitivity and neurotransmitters such as dopamine, noradrenaline, oxytocin, GABA and serotonin. In addition to 5-HTTLPR, which is involved in serotonin transport, the polymorphic DRD4 gene also appears to be a candidate. That gene codes for the dopamine receptor D4 and thus determines how well dopamine is passed on in the brain. Dopamine is a neurotransmitter that plays a role in attention, rewarding and motivation. DRD4 consists of a number of repeats, ranging from 2 to 11. The most common variant is 4-repeat. People with the 7-repeat variant have a less efficient dopamine receptor. The study by Moore and Depue shows that these people display increased environmental sensitivity.[15]

A single high sensitivity gene cannot be singled out, if that were even possible. It is always a combination of multiple genes and the environment. The DRD4 7 repeat gene appears to be related to environmental sensitivity which lies at the heart of high sensitivity, as well as the s/s variant of the polymorphic gene 5-HTTLPR. Because there is a link between high sensitivity and certain genetic differences, it is called a temperament. A temperament is a trait that is deeply rooted in a person's biological 'makeup' and is therefore quite unchangeable.

1.5 SUMMARY

The trait of high sensitivity was first described by Elaine Aron, but other researchers have also found differences between the ways in which people react to new situations and to what extent they are influenced by their environment. Highly sensitive people are very sensitive to the environment in which they find themselves.

High sensitivity is a trait characterized by a great sensitivity to stimuli, a profound processing thereof and an intense reaction to it. Highly sensitive people think before they act. They suffer a lot from negative situations, but also benefit greatly from positive circumstances.

It is not possible to identify a single high sensitivity gene, because an interplay of several genes and the environment always exists. What is clear is that the s/s genotype of the 5-HTTLPR gene is closely associated with high sensitivity and a connection seems to exist with the occurrence of the 7-repeat variant of the DRD4 gene.

CHAPTER 2

Highly Sensitive People

Katie sat very quietly next to her mother on the sofa. It was as if a different child had suddenly appeared. She had just been playing happily with my son. They found each other while playing pretend, creating their own story with anything at hand. Where other six-year-olds played more side by side, not always knowing how to compromise, Katie sensed other children very well and tuned in to them. Whenever she felt safe, she would show her wise and imaginative side. Fortunately, Katie felt safe with us. Her mother, I'll call her Fiona, is a friend of mine and Katie often came to play.

The reason she was leaning shyly against her mother was that she heard, or perhaps especially felt, that Fiona was talking about the conversation she had had at school. The teacher was worried about Katie. She seemed to find reading very difficult and was often alone during break time. When the teacher encouraged her to play, she often started to cry. I saw various emotions on my friend's face: disbelief, concern, fear, but also anger and incomprehension. 'The teacher said she should go back to kindergarten. But she has been reading books since she was five. And she plays together just fine when she's here. What's wrong? What am I doing wrong? I'm doing well with her, right? Then why is her teacher so concerned about this?' She asked me in despair.

I had already read a little about high sensitivity and could understand Katie's behavior. 'You're doing fine,' I said. Katie is a girl who can already do a lot. She can read fine already. And she can play well with others. But only if the environment is safe for her. If the environment is new, for example with a different teacher, classroom or classmates, she needs time to adjust. I think she just needs to get used to it, don't you think?'
Fiona's face changed. I saw all kinds of memories go through her mind. Times when Katie had also been upset. Cried inconsolably. Did not want to do anything. Until it felt safe and she joined in anyway.
Fiona pulled her daughter close and gave her a kiss. Apparently that was a sign, because Katie walked back to the Legos to get back into her pretend game.

If you indicate at school that you are left-handed, then it is clear to teachers what that means and what needs to be arranged: a suitable pen and scissors for left-handed people. If you say that you are highly sensitive, it is different. Not everyone knows what this means, let alone what effect it has on daily life. In this chapter, I will give more insight into this.

2.1 INSIGHT INTO THE LIFE OF A HIGHLY SENSITIVE PERSON

How to gain better insight into how highly sensitive people experience daily life than by letting them speak for themselves? In my own search for knowledge about high sensitivity, I noticed that scientific articles were quite abstract, while books often merely highlighted the author's life. I was curious about how the average highly sensitive person perceived his or her trait. Since there was no such information available yet, I launched a number of studies myself (see box).

Researching high sensitivity

In 2014 I asked parents of highly sensitive children to share their experiences. Nearly 650 parents – an unexpectedly high number – completed my survey. In that survey, I first asked a number of questions based on the HSP scale, so it would be clear which children were indeed highly sensitive. After correction (the children who turned out to not be highly sensitive were removed from the file), 635 participants remained. The results provided insight into the characteristics of high sensitivity: To which stimuli are the children sensitive? How do they process information in depth? In addition, I asked about the problems they were experiencing. This study showed that more than half of the highly sensitive children had difficulty sleeping and experienced problems at school. These large numbers prompted us to take a deeper look at these problems.

At the end of 2014, I initiated a second study among parents of highly sensitive children. More than 750 parents answered my questions, of which 722 turned out to have a highly sensitive child after assessment of the HSP items. This research more explicitly illustrated where the problems lie. For example, 37% of the highly sensitive children appear to have difficulty falling asleep. I also asked about characteristics, such as extraversion and being strong-willed, in addition to high sensitivity, and was therefore able to detect groups of children who experienced problems more often and therefore need extra attention in the supervision. I published the results of these studies in my book *Hoogsensitieve kinderen; praktische leidraad voor ouders en professionals* (Highly sensitive children; a practical guide for parents and professionals).[1]

In 2015, more than 2000 adults shared their experiences with high sensitivity by completing a survey. After correction, 1977 participants remained. The survey mapped how highly sensitive people experience their sensitivity: which senses are heightened, how strongly they are influenced by atmosphere, which effect the social group has on them and which elements of depth of processing are recognized by them? I then asked them about their experiences in the field of work, social contacts and relationships. To illustrate, the results show that many highly sensitive people, in all areas of life, sense the mood of others. A striking 77% indicated to require a good atmosphere to be able to work pleasantly. This prompted a new study.

In 2017 I launched the study HSP and work (stress). More than 1,500 highly sensitive people completed the survey, of which 1,459 remained after correction. In this study, I honed in on the question of what highly sensitive people need to be able to function well at work. A pleasant atmosphere was at the top of the list, above aspects such as a quiet workspace, autonomy, career opportunities, or flexible working hours, which ended much lower on the list.
In 2018 I replicated this study in over twenty countries. In addition to the Dutch study, there was an English, Spanish, Portuguese, Italian, Finnish, Norwegian and Russian version. More than 5,500 HSPs participated in over twenty countries. These international results confirm that highly sensitive people worldwide experience the same aspects of high sensitivity.

On www.hoogsensitief.nl you will find several blogs about the results of both the Dutch and the international study HSP and work (stress).

My research illustrates that problems can arise in all areas of life. Almost all highly sensitive children (97%) experience problems in one or more areas. For example, 55% experience sleep problems, 50% have problems at school, 42% struggle when playing with friends and 40% experience eating issues.[2]

Highly sensitive adults also experience problems in different areas of life. I asked them whether they often feel confined in any way in terms of social contacts. To this, 40% said yes. They regularly experience a degree of incapacity when it comes to social contacts. In addition, 38% often feel physically unable to do something, 35% feel incapacitated in relationships and 34% at work. How this incapacity manifests itself differs from person to person. Where one person avoids activities as a result of this, others do participate while feeling very uncomfortable in doing so.

The issues often stated by highly sensitive adults and children include fatigue, pain issues, concentration problems, being emotional often, feeling different, having difficulty with changes, irritability, being overwhelmed by groups of people, feeling the sorrow of others, avoiding tasks or activities, experiencing a lot of stress and difficulty to unwind and a 'full head'.

However, these issues are not an inseparable part of high sensitivity. It can be compared to left-handedness: illegible handwriting is not necessarily a part of this, because there are left-handed people who can write clearly and neatly. But because left-handers have to put their hand over what has already been written and pens are tuned to right-handers, problems often arise with writing. It is the same with high sensitivity. This characteristic can cause issues, but this is not always the case.
In my book *Hoogsensitieve kinderen* (Highly sensitive children) I reveal the benefits of mapping the underlying factors of the concerned behavior. Concentration problems arise, for example, because the highly

sensitive person becomes overstimulated by all the impressions surrounding him. To help parents change their child's behavior, I distinguish Trait – Effect – Need – Behavior. In this example: the trait high sensitivity leads to the effect of overstimulation. That can trigger the need to shut down your brain. As a result, you can no longer concentrate on your task. Through this analysis, the causes of the experienced problems become clearer and thus also the possible solutions. Three important effects often arise that explain many of the experienced issues. These are overstimulation, fear of failure, and low self-esteem.

Overstimulation

Overstimulation indicates an imbalance between the incoming stimuli and the ability to process them. When the brain can no longer handle the number of stimuli, it intervenes. For example, by 'getting overheated'. This is often experienced as a blackout: you are no longer able to use your mental capacities. The accompanying emotions are often released in the form of tantrums or crying fits. The brain can also shut itself off from new information. In that case, what is going on is no longer perceived and the need to withdraw arises. The person appears apathetic to loved ones.

In highly sensitive people, overstimulation may occur more quickly because they perceive more stimuli and lose more energy due to the intense processing of these stimuli. As a result, the supply is greater while the processing capacity is smaller, quickly resulting in an overload.

For highly sensitive people, becoming overstimulated is an often recurring problem that has a major impact on their lives. Yet, becoming overstimulated is not inextricably linked to high sensitivity. There are also highly sensitive people who are hardly ever overstimulated. My own research shows that 44% of highly sensitive employees say they become overstimulated at work one or more times a day, while 14% are only overstimulated less than once a week.[3] 43% of the highly sensitive children are regularly overstimulated at school.

The problems that can arise from overstimulation are diverse. Highly sensitive employees worldwide mention these issues: too many thoughts (76%), fatigue (75%), need to withdraw (68%), difficulty concentrating (68%), avoiding contact with others (68%), irritability (66%), negative thoughts (64%), self-criticism (63%), forgetfulness (62%), sleeping problems (59%), and (head) pain issues (50%). In addition, they indicate that they feel restless (43%), make more mistakes (41%), and perform less well (41%).[4]

Fear of failure

> *'Since last year he has gone from being a positive little boy with a lot of confidence to a boy who thinks he's the dumbest boy in the whole world. He often makes negative comments, saying he doesn't want to live anymore, didn't want to be born, etc.'* – Mother of a highly sensitive 5-year-old boy

> *'I am quite insecure and always afraid that people don't like me. Sometimes I'm even afraid that my friends pretend to like me. And I can also think very badly about myself.'* – Highly sensitive 14-year-old girl

> *'I'm always afraid that I'm not doing something well enough or that I'm not good enough. I'd rather write than talk. When I write I can correct mistakes, when I talk I can't.'* – Highly sensitive 63-year-old man

Depth of processing, one of the main components of high sensitivity, includes the desire to make the best possible choices: the optimal-option-ambition (see chapter 7). The highly sensitive brain is strongly attuned to (the interests of) others. It likes to do well in the social context. And there is always something that did not go perfectly. We call the strong desire to prevent mistakes fear of failure. A fear that can paralyze us when we have to perform or face new situations.

According to their parents, more than 60% of highly sensitive children experience fear of failure. Highly sensitive children already exhibit this behavior from the age of 4.[5] The percentage is also high among adults, 64% indicate to experience fear of failure.

Fear of failure can affect school and work as well as social relationships. The quotes above illustrate this. In my research, 67% of HSPs indicate they would like to be less critical of themselves, but struggle with this on a daily basis. It affects their behavior at work and in relationships.
There are two types of fear of failure: passive and active fear of failure. The passive form leads people to avoid situations or tasks. They try to get out of tasks, start late, do not discuss problems, and avoid confrontation. With the active form, someone cannot stop a task because the result is not yet perfect. He puts too much time into a project, finds it difficult to accept mistakes (also from others), and is always looking for a better option. This perfectionism is recognizable to many HSPs: 60% of HSPs worldwide identify with this.
The fear of failure percentage is especially high in introverted, reticent highly sensitive children (85% versus 60% of all highly sensitive children).[6] They often have the passive form: they refuse to try new sports or hobbies, like to stick to the puzzle they already know and do not easily rely on other children. These children need guidance in order not to lag behind in their cognitive, physical, or social development.

Low self-esteem or little self-confidence

Having little self-confidence or low self-esteem means that you value yourself less than others. While fear of failure is about your own *abilities* – 'I probably can't do that' – low self-esteem is about who you *are*: 'I'm not good enough.' Obviously, the two influence each other.
Half of the highly sensitive children have low self-esteem, as do half of the adults.[7] 45% of adults find it difficult to deal with their lack of self-confidence in everyday life. Partly due to this, almost half find it difficult to stand up for themselves: 41% at work, 45% in social contacts,

and 33% in romantic relationships. Having little confidence in yourself has consequences for social and cognitive development and for your own identity.

2.2 TALENTS

Although high sensitivity also entails talents and advantages (I will discuss these in detail in the next chapters), they often seem to be somewhat neglected. This has three reasons.

First of all, the negative effects are quite drastic. A highly sensitive person who is overstimulated on a daily basis, feels held back by his fear of failure and feels too little self-confidence to seek help from loved ones, has a hard time staying afloat. Statistics show that this is no exception: 64% of HSPs have trouble dealing with their own intense or strong emotions and 49% struggle every day to simply survive. This daily struggle often makes them blind to their talents.

In the second place, these negative effects are probably more common than a few decades ago, making the talents even less visible. Today, there are many more stimuli in our daily lives. More is demanded of us (both at work and in social contacts) and stimuli from the digital world have been added on, which continuously enter our consciousness via beeps from our smartphones. The more stimuli, the faster someone can become overstimulated. The more demands, the more often fear of failure can be triggered. As a result, more and more attention is paid to the difficult aspects of high sensitivity at the expense of the associated qualities.

Finally, the benefits of high sensitivity have shifted to the background because our societal norms seem to have changed. While waiting for your turn was once worth a compliment, nowadays being able to stand up for yourself is applauded. Rapid decision-making seems to win over careful consideration. In her book *Quiet,* Susan Cain shows that extroverted qualities in today's society have an advantage over the more introverted talents. This has major consequences for work and relationships. She lobbies to restore the introverted qualities. But until that actually happens, people who do not meet the current ideal picture will experience consequences. They feel inadequate, which is detrimental to their self-confidence.

What do highly sensitive people themselves say about their talents? Most HSPs experience empathy as their greatest quality. 5500 HSPs worldwide stated to have the following talents:[8]

Empathy (85%)
Reliable (83%)
Sense of responsibility (83%)
Strong intuition (79%)
Good listener (78%)
Open-minded (76%)
Caring (76%)
Creative thinking (70%)
Attention to detail (70%)
Able to see the big picture (69%)
Sense of humor (65%)
Analytical ability (59%)
Organizational talent (58%)
Easy to make contact (53%)
Conscientious (53%)
Imagination (51%)

Talents such as persuasiveness, perseverance, being able to process a lot of information and assessing risks are mentioned by far fewer HSPs. The image that emerges from the above list is that of the loyal employee who closes the gaps for the team, who pays attention to people, notices and adjusts small subtleties, and comes up with new ideas. Thus, a very valuable colleague and employee.

2.3 SUMMARY

If the trait of high sensitivity is not properly understood, daily problems experienced by highly sensitive people may also be misinterpreted. Katie had no trouble reading and was perfectly able to play together with others. The new teacher, the changed daily schedule, and a larger class were major changes for her, however. As a result, she became overstimulated almost every day. This is the result of an imbalance between the number of stimuli to be processed and the available processing capacity.

Overstimulation often causes issues such as tantrums and crying fits, but can also cause withdrawal from social contact, mental problems (such as a reduced ability to concentrate), and physical symptoms (such as headaches). Other common effects are fear of failure and low self-esteem. These effects sometimes overshadow the many talents that are also associated with high sensitivity.

CHAPTER 3

The Brain

'It is with the brain that we think and have a real understanding of things. It is with the brain that we see and hear, discerning the ugly from the beautiful, the good from the evil and the pleasant from the unpleasant.'[1]
This statement is from the Morbo Sacro – a scripture from the early fourth century BC, thousands of years before we could study the functioning of the brain with brain scans.

The more scientists discover, the more they realize how little we know about how the brain works. Despite the limitations in knowledge, I think it is important to discuss a few concepts here, in order to make the results of research into the highly sensitive brain more comprehensible. To that end, I will first provide a brief overview of the anatomy of the brain. Then I will cover some relatively new discoveries.
I am nowhere near complete in my descriptions of the brain. Firstly, that is impossible, and secondly, there are so many different views that it would be more confusing than enlightening if I were to cover them all.

3.1 ANATOMY

The brain is a network of billions of intercommunicating neurons that exchange information via neurotransmitters. Neurons, or nerve cells, are cells that specialize in receiving, processing, and transmitting information to and from other cells in the body. Passing on such a signal is also called 'firing'. These neurons together form parts of the brain. These parts are arranged in different ways by different scientists.[2]
Here, I will mention several parts of the brain that are important for understanding the following chapters. All areas of the brain are also summarized in the index, which can easily be consulted while reading.

The brain stem

In evolutionarily terms, this is the oldest part of the brain. Reptiles also have a brain stem. It is located at the end of the spinal cord, in the core of the brain and controls a number of vital bodily functions.

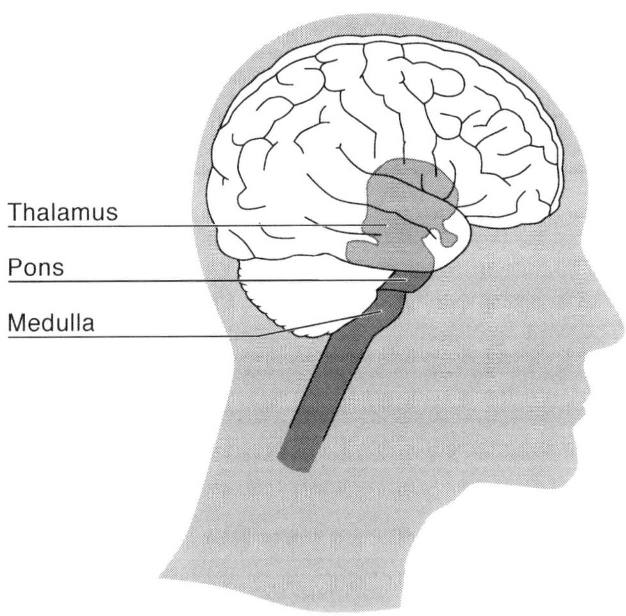

Figure 3.1 The brain stem

The **brain stem** contains the **medulla** and the **pons**. The medulla regulates many vital body functions and reflex movements, such as breathing, heart rate, vomiting, saliva production, coughing and sneezing. The pons (meaning 'bridge') guides the nerve pathways to the other side of the body, enabling the left hemisphere to control the right side muscles and the right hemisphere the left side. The pons plays a role in the alertness and coordination of motor movements.

The **thalamus** (this term is derived from the Greek word for 'inner chamber') receives all visual, auditory, and taste stimuli and sends this information to areas in the cerebral cortex (see below) for further processing. The cortex also sends information back to the thalamus so it can focus attention to certain stimuli. Scent does not travel through the thalamus, but directly to the concerned area in the cerebral cortex. The thalamus is sometimes considered as part of the brain stem. It is located in the center of the brain, between the cerebellum and cerebrum (see below), and forms the top end of the brain stem. The thalamus and the hypothalamus (see below) together are called 'diencephalon', or 'interbrain'. Sometimes the thalamus is placed in the limbic system (see below).

Cerebellum

This part is located next to the brain stem and under the cerebrum (see below). It looks a bit like a small copy of the cerebrum: it is just as wrinkled and also has two halves. The **cerebellum** (literally **'little brain'**) attends to locomotion and maintaining balance. This area of the brain is strongly influenced by alcohol: drinking therefore affects your ability to walk straight. In addition, the cerebellum is important for correcting movements and in tasks that rely on working memory. It is also involved in timing; for example, estimating how fast a rhythm is. Finally, it plays a role in aspects of learning and conditioning, such as learning certain behaviors by means of punishments and rewards.

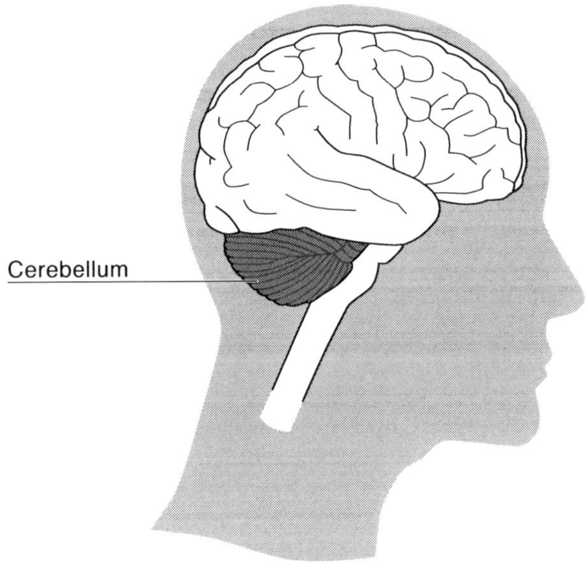

Figure 3.2 The cerebellum

Cerebrum

The **cerebrum** contains the limbic system, the basal ganglia, and the cerebral cortex. These are discussed below.

Limbic system

The name of this part of the brain is derived from the Latin word for border: the **limbic system** borders the brain stem. The cerebral cortex surrounds the limbic system. The limbic system consists of the hypothalamus, hippocampus, amygdala, and cingulate cortex.

The **hypothalamus**, together with the thalamus, is also referred to as the interbrain – the diencephalon. It regulates hunger, thirst, aggression, body temperature, and sexual urges. In addition, the hypothalamus is an important part of the stress system. It connects the nervous system and the hormone system and stimulates, among other things, the production of stress hormones such as cortisol and (nor)adrenaline.

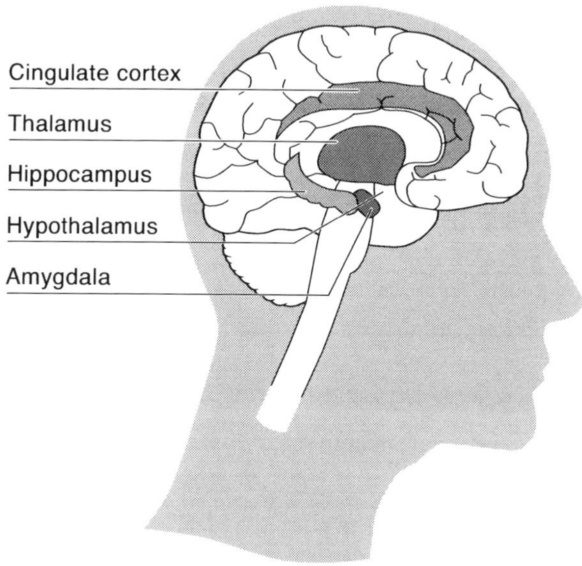

Figure 3.3 The limbic system

The **hippocampus** is shaped a bit like a seahorse; the name is therefore derived from the Latin word for this. There is one in each hemisphere of the brain. The hippocampus plays a role in memory: the storage and retrieval of experiences. It stores the context of experiences. It is also involved in spatial memory, such as learning to navigate through a city. To illustrate, taxi drivers in large cities have been found to have a larger hippocampus, especially if they are experienced drivers.[3] The hippocampus thus grows, among other things, by completing complicated navigation tasks. It shrinks when a person has experienced prolonged stress. As a result, it becomes more difficult to remember the context of a memory and you are less able to put situations into perspective.

The **amygdala** ('almond') evaluates emotional information. Such an almond-shaped brain part exists in each hemisphere. In the past, the amygdala was defined as a fear center, but its function is much broader.[4] It is involved in emotion and motivation. The amygdala gives emotional meaning to information, both incoming sensory information and information from memory. In the latter case, it interacts with the hippocampus. If the hippocampus does not work properly – for example during a period of prolonged stress – the emotional colorization of a memory by the amygdala dominates the relativistic ability of the hippocampus. You then react more emotionally.

The **cingulate cortex** is wrapped around the corpus callosum which connects the two hemispheres of the brain. The cingulate cortex plays a role in the perception of emotional and cognitive conflict. The front part is called the anterior cingulate cortex (ACC). This area will later be discussed in detail as the social-error radar: wondering whether you will be socially rewarded or punished. It also becomes active when experiencing physical and social pain (for example, due to exclusion).[5]

Basal ganglia

The **basal ganglia**, the limbic system, and the interbrain are collectively referred to as the subcortex: that what lies beneath the cortex. The basal ganglia lie beneath the cerebral cortex and form a ring around the thalamus. The area plays a role in movement (Parkinson's disease, for example, is associated with it) and in experiencing reward.

In the **ventral striatum**, part of the basal ganglia, the emotional value of an action is determined. It plays a role in positive sensations such as desire, motivation, passion, and satisfaction and tangibly in addiction behavior, sexuality, gaming, and emotions aroused by listening to music. In addition, it also becomes active in case of anticipated rewards. The prospect of satisfaction produces activity in this area.
People also experience social stimuli as a reward. Looking at a photograph of your mother or partner activates this area. Another part that will be discussed later is the ventral tegmental area (VTA). This area is specifically aimed at registering whether an event is rewarding or disappointing.[6] The dopamine-related reward system starts in this area.[7]

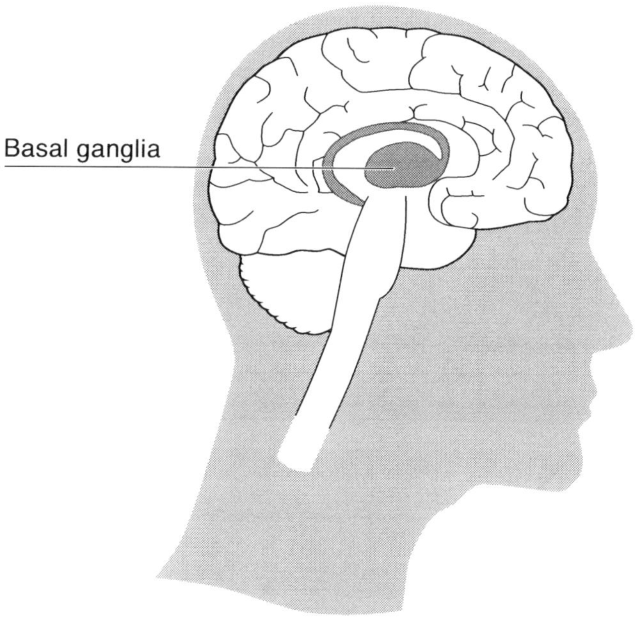

Figure 3.4 The basal ganglia

Therefore, it plays a role in addictive behavior, in motivation, but also in intense feelings of love.

Cerebral cortex

Most of our brain is the **cerebral cortex**. This is the outer layer directly under the skull that makes up two-thirds of the total mass of our brain. The cerebral cortex resembles a walnut due to the many wrinkles. The cortex consists of five lobes:

a. the **frontal lobe**. It is located at the front. The front section of the frontal lobe is called the prefrontal cortex (PFC). The frontal lobe is involved in many different functions:
   - planning (fine) movement and regulation of motor functions, such as picking up your phone;
   - working memory: your ability to remember recent things, such as where you put your smartphone;

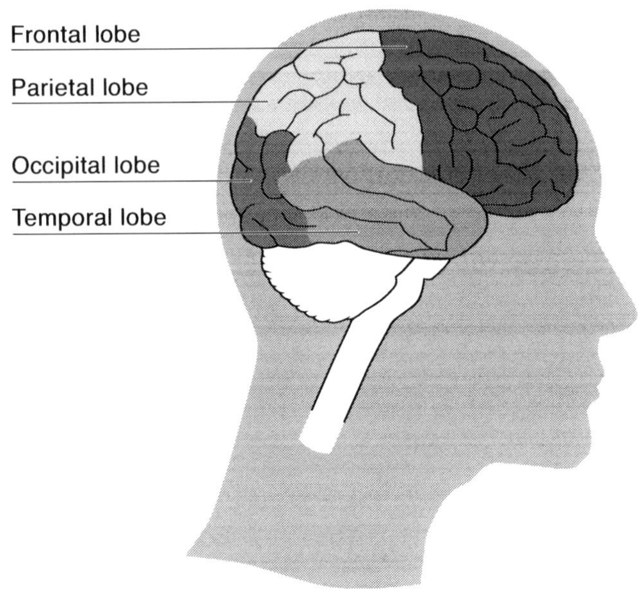

Figure 3.5 The cerebral cortex

- being able to exercise cognitive control over what you do or say, for example not saying everything that comes to mind;
- some emotional functions, in conjunction with other areas of the brain;
- making decisions: being able to see what the effect is and which decision will have the best result given the situation. This is also referred to as higher-order decision making: considering whether you want to go skiing for a weekend or save money for a long vacation in the summer. If this area is not well developed, you make impulsive choices.

Two areas of the prefrontal cortex will often be discussed in the following chapters:

- the dorsolateral prefrontal cortex (DLPFC). The term 'dorsolateral' refers to the location in the prefrontal cortex: the top and outside of the brain. The DLPFC regulates higher-order cognitive

processes: more difficult rational tasks such as decision making, complex tasks and executive functions;[8]
- the medial prefrontal cortex (mPFC). This area is part of the social brain. It is active when judging others, judging yourself in relation to others, but also when empathizing with others.[9]

b. the **parietal lobe**. This is located behind the frontal lobe on top of your head. This area regulates and senses all motor and sensory activity in the body. The parietal lobe consists of:
   - the primary motor cortex. This area regulates the movements of different parts of the body, such as the arm, hand, and finger;
   - the primary somatosensory cortex. This area represents the sensations that take place in the concerned areas, so that you actually feel pain in your finger or a tingling in your arm.

A kind of map exists in both cortexes, allowing the brain to register where the information from the body originates and allowing you to pinpoint that you have hurt your right knee. Information regarding motor skills and the sensations of the body processed by the parietal lobe are important for proper steering of the body. As a result, your body knows what to do when it bumps its knee.
In addition, this lobe also contributes to the processing of visual and auditory information, in which other areas of the brain are actually more specialized. After all, when you hear a vehicle approaching – for your own safety – it is important to know from which direction it is approaching and what position your body is in. The brain then passes that information on to the areas that control movement, so you can make the right movement in time to get out of the way.

c. the **occipital lobe**. This is located at the back of your head. It processes visual information. Light, which enters through the eyes, is sent through the visual cortex to areas in the occipital lobe, which

processes the color, movement, shape, etc. This creates images of the outside world.
This area cooperates a lot with other areas. The parietal lobe determines the position of an object. When stepping on to an escalator for example, information about the escalator and information about your body position are required to get on the escalator in one smooth step. Furthermore, the occipital lobe, in conjunction with the temporal regions, makes memories visual.

d. the **temporal lobe.** It is located on the side of your head, at the height of your temples, and processes auditory information. When your phone rings, the sound is processed in this area. An important part, the left auditory cortex, is essential in understanding spoken text. This allows you to follow the telephone conversation. Recognizing faces, in this example the photo id of the caller, also takes place in this lobe – and not, as you might expect, in the occipital lobe, which pro-

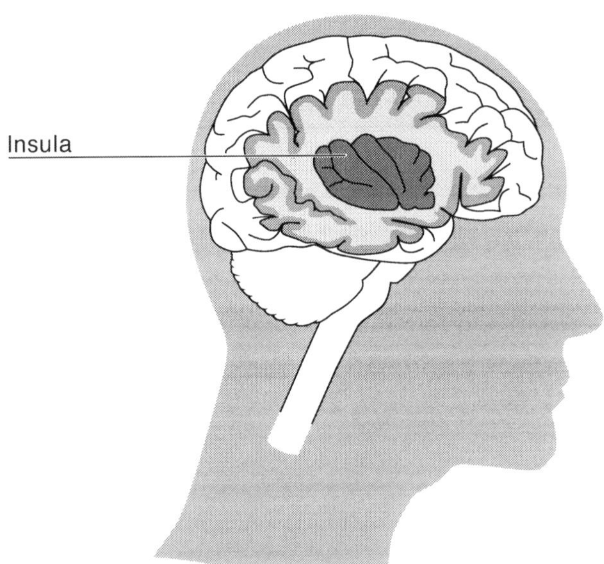

Figure 3.6 The insula

cesses visual information. The temporal lobe also plays a role in the perception of movement and in emotional and rewarding behavior.

e. the **insula**. This fifth – less known – lobe is located behind the temporal lobe.[10] It is connected to many other areas and probably specializes in monitoring bodily sensations in conjunction with emotional and empathic processes. For example, this lobe ensures that you perceive hunger, that you feel your heart rate increase, and that you experience (emotional) disgust – in short, that you are aware of your own being. The insula also plays a major role in attuning to other people[11] and in decision-making[12] and is therefore seen as an important link between cognition and feeling.[13]

3.2 BRAIN NETWORKS

The different areas of the brain work together. We call a group of brain areas that are functionally connected a brain network. For example, the sensorimotor network, the language network, and the visual network can all be distinguished. There are three networks that are especially important for a better understanding of cognitive functioning.[14] These are the central executive network (CEN), the default mode network (DMN) and the salience network (SN).

Salience network

'Salience' means distinctiveness. This network consists of brain areas that are mainly activated by distinctive events in the environment. According to Menon and Udin (2010), this network detects salient events, mobilizes attentional and memory functions, and activates physiological activity required for the event. A malfunctioning salience network is related to schizophrenia and hallucinations, whereby the signals from within are perceived more strongly than the events in the environment.

The central brain parts of this network are the anterior cingulate cortex (ACC) and, especially, the insula. Within the salience network, the insula ensures suppression of the default mode network (see below) and activation of the central executive network (see below).

Central executive network

The brain areas of the central executive network are activated during cognitively demanding tasks, for example when you have to retain and process information in your working memory, as is the case with mental arithmetic.[15] Or when you have to assess situations and make decisions in order to achieve a goal. The main brain areas of this network are the dorsolateral prefrontal cortex and the posterior parietal cortex (PPC).

Default mode network

The default mode network is the only brain network that becomes active when no task is being performed. This area was actually discovered by accident. In studies with fMRI scans, brain activity is measured, but the scan also shows activity between assignments. For a long time this was considered to be static noise, but we now know the brain is also active during periods of rest. When we are not performing any activity, the DMN will turn on. If attention is needed for something important, brain activity in this area must be low. Therefore, when this occurs, the salience network suppresses activity in the DMN. The stronger that activity is suppressed, the better your performance will be.[16]

The default mode network consists of several brain areas:[17]

- the ventromedial prefrontal cortex. This is an area in the medial prefrontal cortex – the social brain – involved in socially positioning yourself in relation to others;
- the posterior cingulate cortex. This area is active in autobiographical memory and self-assessment;
- the medial temporal lobes. These are also involved in (autobiographical) memory;

- the temporo-parietal junction (TPJ), which is involved in empathy; and
- the angular gyrus (AG), which plays a role in processing language and understanding metaphors.

Thus, the DMN is active when people think without a specific task, namely with autobiographical memory, thinking about the future, empathy, and moral decision-making. It actually simulates what the world could be like.[18] This will help you prepare for future events. You do need 'concepts' to be able to simulate. This activity is therefore not yet visible in babies.[19]

An important discovery is that the DMN is more active when intense emotions are felt. In a study by Raz and colleagues, respondents were shown several movie scenes: two clips evoking grief (from *Sophie's Choice* and *Stepmom*), excerpts from *The Ring 2* and *The X-Files* to provoke fear, and a clip from the documentary *Avenge but one of my two eyes* to trigger anger.[20] People who felt an emotion very intensely were found to have more activity in their DMN.

Mirror neurons

One last brain discovery I want to mention here is that of mirror neurons. These were discovered by Rizzolatti. Using brain scans, Rizzolatti and his colleagues examined macaques.[21] They studied what happens in the brain when the monkeys grabbed and picked up objects. The story goes that one of the researchers picked up an object during break time, while a monkey whose brain was currently being scanned was watching. The scans showed that the same areas of the brain became active while watching as when they picked up an object themselves. At first, the researchers thought there was something wrong with the equipment, but then they felt they were onto something. They let researchers pick up a raisin and place it on a tray so the monkey could pick up the raisin afterward. The monkey's neurons in the primary mo-

tor cortex were similarly active when he saw the researcher picking up the raisin as when he picked it up himself. Indeed, mirror neurons are neurons that respond to their own actions as well as to the observed actions of others.
To test how this works exactly, Rizzolatti also looked at the activity in the monkey's brain when a researcher placed a raisin on the tray. This did not appear to result in increased activity in the brain. Then he let the monkey watch a researcher pretend to pick up a raisin or pick up food with a tool. Neither action resulted in activity in the monkey brain. Only the direct observation of picking up or grasping food or objects led to the same activity in that brain area as when the monkey picked up the food itself. This is how Rizzolatti demonstrated the existence of mirror neurons.

Important brain areas in relation to mirror neurons are the premotor area, the inferior parietal lobe (IPL), the insula, the temporo-parietal junction (TPJ), and the inferior frontal gyrus (IFG).[22] The first mainly contains the motor neurons. In the other areas, the mirror neurons involved in the transfer of emotions are found. People with highly activated mirror neurons are quick to cry when they see someone else cry. They experience the same emotions as the other, but that is only the case when they understand the other's perspective.[23]

Mirror neurons are also referred to as 'intention detectors' because they only go into effect when the purpose of the action is clear.[24] Idle actions, such as pretending to pick up a raisin in the example above, do not trigger brain activation. The same goes for emotions. Only when you can connect with another person's situation, will you be able to experience the same emotions.

This is also known as theory of mind, or mentalizing: being able to put yourself in the shoes of others and to understand their intentions and situation. In addition to feeling emotions, this is considered to be an important part of empathy. In order to empathize with the other, you have to be able to feel what the other feels and understand it. In various theories these two parts of empathy are given different names. Zaki and Ochsner talk about mirroring versus mentalizing.[25] Simon Baron-Cohen and colleagues, among others, distinguish between affective empathy (feeling emotions) and cognitive empathy (being able to put yourself in the shoes of the others).[26] Within research, this cognitive element of empathy is mainly linked to the temporo-parietal junction (TPJ).[27]

Mirror neurons and the default mode network support each other in this. Research where people were asked to empathize with others who were brushing their teeth, drinking coffee, or eating ice cream yielded an interesting result. When asked to imagine *how* the other did this, the mirror neurons in the motor areas became active. When asked *why* these people conducted these actions, the DMN was triggered strongly. Thus, the DMN is also involved in interpreting the purpose of actions. It is based on previous experiences. In this sense, it connects past, present and future.[28]

3.3 HOW EMOTIONS ARISE

Scientists, each with their own perspective and specialty, have only just begun to discover the brain. Some scientists think in terms of domain specification. They look for brain areas that specialize in processing a specific type of information, for example an area that is only active when it recognizes faces, or a fear center. They assume that each part of the brain has its own function. Other scientists are looking more at the cooperation between different brain areas. They believe that no single area fulfills only one function on its own. For example, they look for specialized networks of brain areas. A final approach goes one step further and even states that specialized networks do not exist.[29]

As a result, some research results contradict or appear to contradict each other. One thing is certain: nothing is certain when it comes to the functioning of our extremely complex brain. The knowledge covered in this book may already be outdated by the time you read this. But we have to start somewhere.

A book that provides an innovative picture of how our brain works is *How emotions are made* by Lisa Feldman Barrett.[30] This distinguished professor of psychology unfolds a whole new vision of emotions. Her work is also important for understanding the highly sensitive brain.
One of the sacred cows she is toppling is the belief that emotions can be 'fingerprinted'. She rejects the domain-specific approach to the brain, because according to her, emotions do not arise in specific brain areas. She argues that emotions do not always manifest themselves in the same way. Meaning, you cannot tell from someone's posture or facial expressions what they feel. One person who is feeling delighted may express this very differently than another. Scientists have tried to read facial expressions for years. Even security services are trying to develop programs to recognize someone's emotions based on micro-expressions.
Feldman Barrett has a more convincing explanation: emotions do not arise because certain areas of the brain are triggered, but because we interpret sensations from our body as emotions. Our brain constructs emotions based on the information it perceives, both internally and externally. Her theory is therefore called theory of constructed emotion.

Prediction loop

Your brain is constantly focused on enabling your body to survive. If it would only respond to situations, the body would be on high alert too late and would be unable to respond to threats adequately. Therefore, your brain continuously transmits predictions. This continuous, intrinsic activity has only recently been discovered and mainly takes place in the default mode network. The body converts these predictions into so-called simulations of sensations and movement. The actual sensations are used to compare, adjust any prediction errors and adapt the body accordingly. Thus, activity in the brain does not start with sensory input, but with a prediction. This prediction simulates an experience (Figure 3.6). For example, if you bite into an apple, the brain is already simulating what you will experience. It predicts a sweet taste and the sound when you bite through the skin.

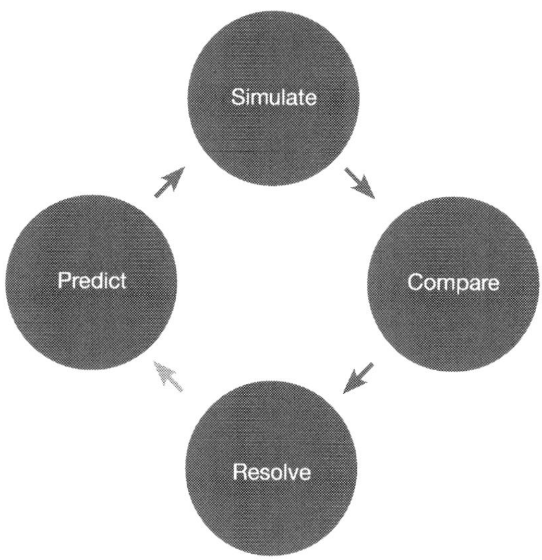

Figure 3.7 The prediction loop (Feldman Barrett, 2017)

That simulation is often correct, but not always. Sometimes the apple turns out to be much more sour than expected, or it has a powdery texture. The sensory input then does not match the prediction. Your brain corrects those errors and responds based on the sensory information. Sometimes you do not notice the differences between the simulation and the sensory stimuli. The errors are not corrected and you react as your brain predicted. This happens, for example, with chronic pain or phantom pain, where the body only responds to predictions and does not correct.[31]

In fact, even visual information works this way. You may expect the visual information in your brain to mainly come from what you see. But 90% of all information that goes to your visual cortex consists of predictions.[32] If you walk into the supermarket and you see a box containing red-colored round objects next to the apples, you assume they are tomatoes. If they turn out to be clown noses, you will not notice until later on.

Feldman Barrett's voluminous book shows how complex our brain is. Different areas of the brain exchange predictions with each other, adapt to each other and activate our immune, nervous, or endocrine systems.

According to Barrett, in order to experience an emotion, the following three universal aspects are necessary: active realism, concepts and social reality.

1 Affective realism

The phenomenon that you perceive what you believe, is called affective realism. Everything you perceive and what you see is colored by your interoceptive networks. These networks, which consist of the default mode and the salience network, perceive the sensations in your body. The feeling produced by these sensations is called affect. Affect consists of two elements: valence, feeling pleasant or unpleasant, and arousal, feeling tense or calm. This is illustrated in Figure 3.8.

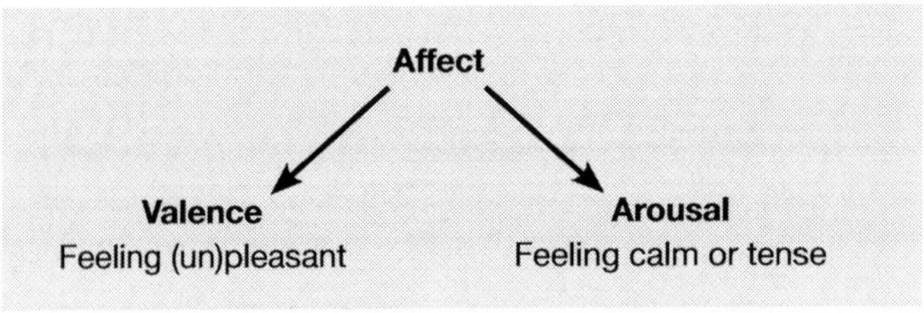

Figure 3.8 Affect: valence and arousal

Because the flow of interoceptive signals always continues, affect is also a continuous flow. When your body is out of balance, affect indicates that something needs to be done, but not what. Your brain looks for explanations. It searches past experiences for events, occurrences, or objects that were of influence. Affect influences your decisions. For example, judges in the US appear to be less likely to release people on bail just before lunch. They interpret their hunger sensation as a negative premonition about the suspect and therefore decide not to allow bail.[33]

2 Concepts

Concepts are words that help you understand the world. Your brain steers your body based on concepts and that is how you stay you alive. They ensure that your body gets the energy it needs. You experience emotions because you give words to the sensations you experience. You cannot experience emotions without emotion concepts.

That may sound strange. If you do not know the word 'sad', is it impossible to feel sad? This can be better understood by considering emotional concepts that you are not familiar with. Different emotions can be found in different cultures. American culture, for example, does not have the same concepts for the Dutch emotions of *voorpret* (anticipatory fun) and *gezelligheid* (conviviality[34]). And have you ever felt the emotion *gigil*? This is a Filipino emotion for the urge to hug or squeeze something that is excruciatingly cute. See the box for more information.

Emotion concepts

Gigil sounds like a made-up emotion to us. It seems very different from 'real' emotions such as anger, fear and sadness.

It is similar to money. Money from other cultures may look 'fake', but it is just as real as our currency. You cannot use foreign money in the US, but you can use concepts from other languages to give meaning to your own sensations.

How about these emotions, for example? Even though there are no English words for them, we have all felt these emotions at one point or another.

Forelsket (Norwegian): intense joy because you are in love
Awumbuk (New Guinea): feeling lazy when a guest has finally left
Age-otori (Japanese): feeling worse after a haircut
Greng jai (Thai): reluctance to accept someone's help because it could cause trouble for the other
Dépaysement (French): dizzying disorientation because you are in an unfamiliar place
L'appel du vide (French): the call of the void, literally. The impulse to do something very dangerous, such as opening the aircraft's emergency exit during a flight
Arigata-meiwaku (Japanese): the feeling of having to feel grateful because someone did something for you, while you did not want that help at all and it has caused you discomfort

Source: Feldman Barrett, 2017; Watt-Smith, 2016

3 Social reality

The third central point in Feldman Barrett's work on emotions is social reality. When your body adjusts itself according to the concepts it has, the concepts at your disposal are crucial. Those concepts are cultural agreements. You accumulate these during your upbringing and your experiences. Many concepts, which people experience as purely physical – such as emotions – are acquired concepts. Our brain converts these concepts into predictions, which then steer the body. If the concepts are too generic or do not fit the situation, false predictions arise. Those wrong predictions can then lead to health problems (see Chapter 9).

Anger

Anger is seen as one of the four basic emotions. These emotions are believed to be recognized and experienced by every human being. However, according to Lisa Feldman Barrett's theory of constructed emotion, that is not the case. She indicates that you interpret sensations in your body as emotions using the concepts you have learned.

She clarifies this by providing examples from different cultures in her book *How emotions are made.* Where the English (and also Dutch) language has one word for anger, Mandarin has five and Russian two. The Inuit do not have a word for anger at all. In Russian, a distinction is made between anger towards a person and anger for more abstract reasons, such as politics. When you are aware of these varieties, you can distinguish between the different forms of anger. In this way, you can prepare your body more adequately for action. Anger at another person calls for different actions than anger at politics, if only because it is easier to talk to a person about your emotion than to something as abstract as politics.

That it is possible to adopt emotional concepts from other cultures, is also apparent from a survey among Turkish immigrants in Belgium. In a situation where a colleague gets in the way of you reaching your goals, the Belgians use the word anger. In Turkey, a mix of anger, shame, guilt and respect is experienced. The longer Turkish immigrants live in Belgium, the more their emotional experience in a similar situation becomes the same as that of the Belgians.

Source: Feldman Barrett, 2017

Lisa Feldman Barrett's work gives us the words to better understand how our brain functions. Those words also help to provide insight into the highly sensitive brain.

3.4 SUMMARY

Our brain is an extremely complex system of tens of billions of neurons, each connected to at least a thousand other neurons. These neurons form brain areas, which together form brain networks that become active when conducting specific tasks. The default mode network deviates from this, as it is active when no task has to be performed.

The recent discovery of mirror neurons makes it clear how people can sense and experience the emotions of others.

Emotions do not arise in specific areas of the brain. The brain constructs emotions by giving words to the sensations it experiences. To this end, the concepts available to the brain are important. Culture and education therefore play a role in the experience of emotions.

CHAPTER 4

Visualizing the Highly Sensitive Brain

After holding the door open for everyone, I was the last to enter the cozy Italian restaurant. The sounds and smells immediately overwhelmed me. All my colleagues were already seated. We had been assigned two tables and there was still one spot available at each table. The choice was mine.

As I took in the situation, I tried to block out the sounds of the music, the chatter of the other patrons, and the yelling from the kitchen. Two colleagues with whom I got along well were seated at the table on the left. One had even become a friend. I would certainly have a pleasant evening sitting there. But that spot was right under the speaker box. Within fifteen minutes, my ears would be hurting. Plus, the chair that stood there looked very uncomfortable. The spot at the other table on the right seemed better: a quieter corner, plus a cushion on the seat.

I already made a move to the right when my eye fell on the person I would be sitting next to: a colleague who was having some issues lately. At times he would shut himself off, other times he would share his frustration extensively. Today, it seemed he had chosen the latter. I felt my shoulders tighten, his negative mood immediately affected me.

I hesitated. Which seat should I choose? The uncomfortable chair next to colleagues with whom I had a good connection? Or the quiet spot next to a colleague who would not stop airing his frustrations? At that second table, there was also an extroverted colleague who did not mince his words. Those two would surely come to a verbal clash. Next to them was our new intern. I noticed he was very uncomfortable. He had no clue how to handle the situation and the tension that seemed to be mounting between the two people next to him. I could take the sting out of that situation. Calm my frustrated colleague with an understanding comment and talk to the extroverted colleague about new developments in the field to avoid a clash. I wanted the intern to have a relaxed evening.

In the meantime, the waiter had walked up to me. With his Italian charm, he pushed back the chair at the left table. My colleague/friend had already poured me a glass of water. I glanced at the intern, who was now huddled over the menu even further, and sat down next to my friend. I was immediately included in their conversation, but was unable to focus on it properly. I heard every word of the now heated discussion behind me and felt how gloomy the intern was becoming. At the same time, the music drowned out my own thoughts.
Even before the food was served, I felt exhausted. At appropriate moments, I laughed at the stories of my tablemates, but I could no longer utter any sentences myself. My head felt as if it were overflowing. Besides, I felt guilty. I had chosen the easy way. I should have turned down this chair and sat at the other table. The discussions there were becoming louder and louder and I knew the dispute would be heated up again the next morning. Hardly any work would be done. I should have sat at the other table and calmed the situation. I focused on my food as a distraction.

4.1 PERSPECTIVE

Why does someone behave in a certain way? There are many answers to this question, depending on the perspective you take. In psychology, for example, there are six main perspectives: the biological, the behaviorist, the developmental, the cognitive, the humanist, and the sociocultural perspective.

Why are children with ADHD, for instance, often hyperactive and easily distracted? If you examine the brain, you can find part of the answer. Shaw (2018) concludes based on longitudinal research that ADHD is related to the growth of white matter in the brain.[1] The speed at which the white matter increases, especially in the cerebellum, is lower at first and higher than average from the age of 8.[2] For executive functions, the size and connectivity of the cerebellum are important; less volume and less connectivity means more problems with executive functions. This explains why it is difficult for young children with ADHD to stay focused and control impulsivity.[3]
Laura Batstra, on the other hand, points to the psychosocial circumstances and believes that many of the problems in hyperactive children can be solved by learning to manage behavior, by both the parent and the child.[4] She maintains a different perspective than Shaw. One answer is not more valuable than the other.

In this book I mainly apply research regarding the functioning of the brain. From this angle, I want to better map the high sensitivity trait. In doing so, some comments are in order.
First, the findings from brain studies provide insight into the high sensitivity trait, but can never paint the full picture. Other perspectives on high sensitivity offer different pieces of the puzzle. It is not my aim to complete the entire puzzle in this book. This book focuses primarily on the highly sensitive brain, a puzzle piece that has remained rather unexplored to this day.

Second, high sensitivity is not a disorder. The brain studies into high sensitivity are not intended to find out where things are 'going wrong'. The researchers did look at differences between highly sensitive and non-highly sensitive people. To make a distinction between these groups, the respondents filled in (a shortened version of) the HSP scale as developed by Elaine Aron.

Thirdly, the interpretation of brain studies is complicated. With each discovery, the brain turns out to be even more complex than we thought. What is currently known, is the result of thorough research. Nevertheless, in a few years' time we may discover that we need to apply nuances to the conclusions we draw now. For this reason, I specify my reasoning as much as possible, allowing new insights to be added more easily and making the insight even more complete.

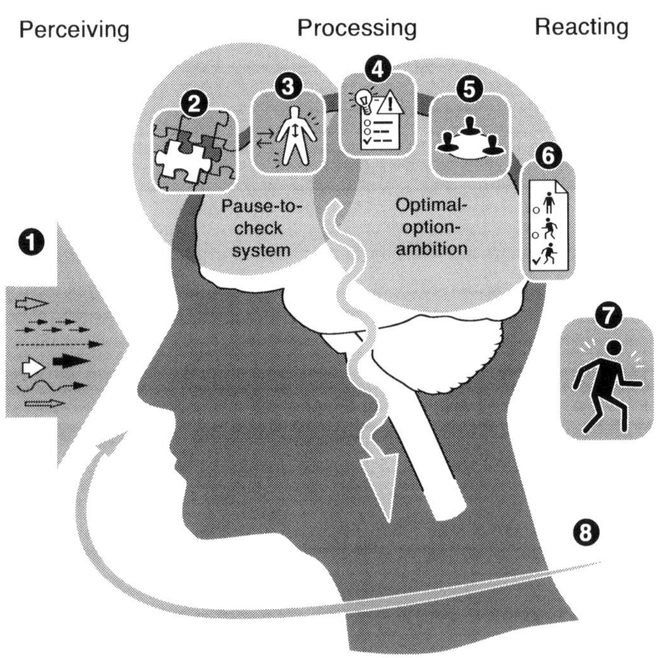

Figure 4.1 Visualizing the Highly Sensitive Brain

In figure 4.1 I have summarized the knowledge about the functioning of the highly sensitive brain. I will explain each part in the following chapters.

4.2 PERCEIVING, PROCESSING, REACTING, AND SELF-REFLECTION

I have divided the functioning of the highly sensitive brain into three main parts: perceiving, processing, and reacting to information from the environment (see figure 4.1).

First of all, the highly sensitive brain perceives more stimuli (number 1 in the figure). This concerns three categories: perceiving through the senses, perceiving emotional signals and perceiving nuances within the surroundings.
Physical stimuli include the sounds of the music and the conversations in the example at the beginning of this chapter. As well as light, taste, and smell: the flickering candles on the tables of the restaurant and the bright lights from the kitchen, the smells of all the different dishes being prepared, and the flavors being slightly different to those at my favorite Italian restaurant (see section 5.1). Second, emotional stimuli are perceived more strongly. In the example, I sense my colleague's bad mood and the intern's uneasiness and am strongly influenced by it (see section 5.2).
Finally, the highly sensitive brain registers subtle details that others miss. For example, I noticed one seat would be more comfortable than the other because my attention was immediately drawn to the speakers and the cushion (section 5.3).

After perception, processing follows. The highly sensitive brain processes the detected stimuli in depth. When I had to choose a seat, I took a moment to weigh my options. I took in the situation before acting. In doing so, I did not only consider the current situation, but combined it with information from previous experiences (number 2 in the figure). I felt my shoulders tighten when I noticed my colleague was in a bad mood (number 3 in the figure). This meant I needed some time to process all the information (the pause-to-check system is explained in Chapter 6).

During that 'pause' to process information before taking action, social considerations mainly play a role. I have called this the optimal-option-ambition (Chapter 7). As I stood there looking at the intern, I imagined the effect a conflict between the two colleagues he was sitting next to would have on him. He was having a hard time fitting in at our department. His talents were not really flourishing, because underlying tensions made him insecure. He did not know how to act. A conflict during a night out would make him lose his balance even further, and perhaps even prompt him to quit. And that would of course also have an effect on current projects. This analysis of risks and opportunities is shown in number 4 in the figure.

In that restaurant I could vividly imagine the effect my choice had on the group. For the overall cohesion in the group, it would be better if I sat at the table on the right. This would alter the interaction at that table and probably improve the atmosphere. But in the back of my mind I considered how my friend would react if I did not sit with her. Would she feel rejected? Would she become closer to our other colleague? Would they develop a bond of friendship, leaving me out? This social error radar is very strong in highly sensitive people (see number 5 in the figure and section 7.2).

While using all this information, I tried to come up with the best action (point 6 in the figure). Should I sit on the left or on the right? During this process I kept observing new details, so the ultimate choice continuously alternated between the two tables (see section 7.3).

After perceiving and processing information, the reaction follows (see number 7 in the figure). This response appears to differ between highly sensitive and non-highly sensitive people. Highly sensitive people experience more intense emotions in the same situation. The intern's cheerless expression touched me deeply and caused stress, while other colleagues barely seemed to notice. I perceived tension and felt exhausted within half an hour. HSPs also experience a higher level of stress than non-highly sensitive people after conducting the same task. All these aspects are discussed in Chapter 8.

The arrow below the head in figure 4.1 (number 8) represents self-reflection. The (re)action does not end the contemplations. The highly sensitive brain also considers its own role in the newly created situation: did I take the right action, what could I have done differently, what could I have done better (see section 8.5)? In my seat next to my friend, my self-reflection quickly turned to self-criticism. I felt I had not made the right choice. I kept replaying all the information I had perceived, to conclude over and over again that I should have been sitting at the other table. These concerns stopped me from having a pleasant conversation over a nice meal.

CHAPTER 5

Perception

In the city where I grew up, there was a carnival every year. Like my friends, I would really look forward to it. I would imagine how much fun I would have at the event weeks prior. Everyone I knew would be there. I would walk through the crowd, arm-in-arm with my friends. We would laugh and scream excitedly on the rides. I could practically smell all the nice scents of the special snacks you could buy, candy that was only available at carnivals back in those days.

On the first day, I would ride my bike to the fairgrounds with my friends, feeling excited. We discussed what we would do first, and after that and after that.

Things took a different turn. After a few minutes, I was suddenly exhausted. The smile had disappeared from my face. I felt gloomy. But did not understand why. After the bumper cars – one of my favorite rides – I felt like I could barely stand on my feet. After just fifteen minutes, I mumbled to my friends, 'Not feeling well, I'm going home.'

At home in bed and safely under the covers I could still see all the carnival lights. The colors were bright, as if I was still standing there. I also saw the faces of the people I had seen. People who were enjoying themselves, but also people who were sad. I could still feel the irritation of a couple I saw arguing over which prize to choose. I saw peers looking disapprovingly at my group of friends. All I could do was cry. Incomprehensible feelings rolled over me. The bells of the bumper cars were still ringing in my ears.

The next day I was afraid to go to school. I was embarrassed I had left early and after a night's sleep I did not understand why I had suddenly left. What should I say to my friends? And how could I convince my parents to let me go to the carnival again? After all, I wanted to have fun.
It took me years to realize why I always felt exhausted in no time whenever I attended a similar event.

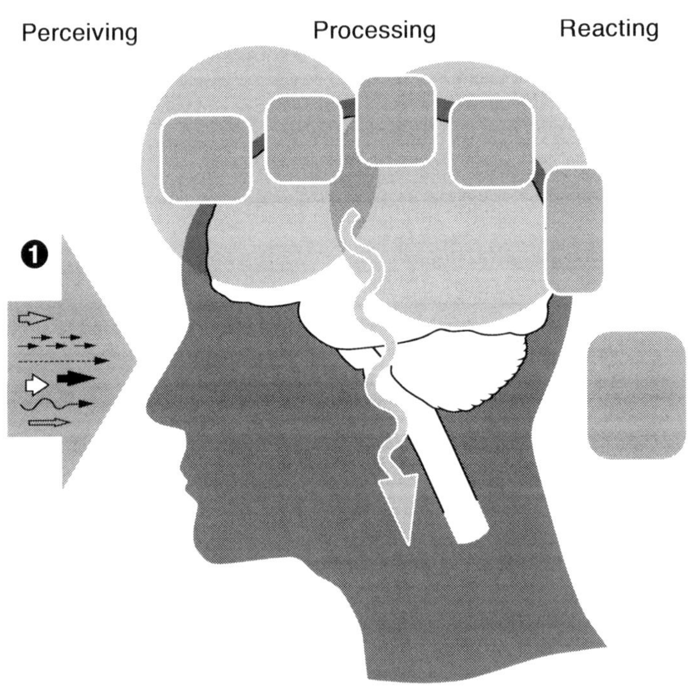

Figure 5.1 The highly sensitive brain: perceiving

This chapter is about perceiving stimuli. Highly sensitive people perceive more when it comes to physical stimuli, emotional signals, and details from their surroundings.

5.1 PHYSICAL STIMULI

Scotswoman Caitlin McNeill was looking for a dress for her daughter's wedding. She sent pictures of the different options to her daughter, asking her which dress to wear. Her daughter's response led to confusion, so Caitlin shared the photo on social media asking, 'What color is this dress?' Social media exploded. One half clearly saw a gold and white dress, while the other half saw a blue and black one. At its peak, over 11,000 tweets per minute were about #TheDress.[1] Team white and gold was convinced of the colors and could not imagine anyone seeing different colors. Team blue and black was equally convinced.
Even after Caitlin McNeill had shown the dress on television, the differences of opinion did not end there. The dress Caitlin wore was black and blue. But the people who saw gold and white hardly believed it.

It is hard to imagine that someone else's perception does not match yours. The image is so clear it seems factual. Perception through the senses, however, differs from person to person. Highly sensitive people often report more intense perception through one or more senses.

In my studies, I asked highly sensitive adults and children which of their senses is more highly developed. I asked them how they perceive sound, light, and smell and asked about their sense of touch and taste. Almost 70% of the more than 700 highly sensitive children said they were bothered by loud noises,[2] this means noise is the most common physical sensitivity. This also applies to adults.[3] For HSPs, loud noises can obstruct concentration or cause such a level of discomfort that they have to leave the room. The second most sensitive sense is the skin. Clothing labels, tight clothing, jewelry, perfumes, sand, and the like are disturbing for many highly sensitive people.[4] The sense of touch also includes pain perception. About half of the highly sensitive children say they are sensitive to pain.[5]

Habituation

Normally our bodies get used to the sounds, smells and lights around us. This process is called sensory adaptation. Receptor cells become less sensitive when a stimulus is presented at the same level for a certain amount of time. Stimuli that do not change in intensity, or some other characteristic, disappear from our consciousness, unless the stimulus is very intense or painful.

When the receptor cells perceive the stimulus less intensely, habituation exists. The body learns that it does not have to respond to the present stimulus. A clothing label, for example, is a stimulus many people may perceive for a while, but then it fades into the background. Or consider the ring on your finger, which you no longer consciously perceive after wearing it for a few days. Habituation is therefore the result of sensory adaptation. The question is whether habituation occurs less quickly for highly sensitive people. Do they continue to perceive stimuli when these have already disappeared into the background for others?

The opposite process is sensitization. With this phenomenon neurons become more sensitive. In this case, offering a stimulus more often leads to an enhanced response. For example, someone who keeps getting a pain stimulus can develop chronic pain.[6] There also seems to be an overflow effect: a lot of pain also creates heightened sensitivity to sounds.

An important concept related to perception is latent inhibition. This mechanism ensures that you are not overwhelmed by everything you perceive. It only selects those stimuli that seem relevant to the moment. The other information is not consciously perceived. This makes it possible, for example, to focus on the person you are talking to during a party. People with a low latent inhibition perceive many more stimuli and are therefore more likely to be overwhelmed.

Differences

Almost all highly sensitive people say they perceive intensely with one or more senses; hearing, vision, sense of smell, taste, and/or touch. They perceive the stimuli more quickly or are more affected by them than other people. No scientific research has yet been conducted into actual sharper or more accurate perception by highly sensitive people. It would be interesting to examine whether the differences in perception are related to high sensitivity.

Linda Bartoshuk has researched the taste system and found differences between people.[7] She indicates that being able to distinguish between flavors is important for our survival. Being able to distinguish bitter flavors – which often contain poison – as well as sweet and fatty products, because they provide us with energy. She found that some people perceive these elements much better than others. According to her, 25% of people taste little, 50% have normal taste, and the remaining 25% are supertasters. This group perceives bitter flavors very strongly and experiences creamy, sweet, and fatty flavors more intensely. They also appear to experience oral pain more strongly. The differences are genetically detectable. It has not been studied whether highly sensitive people always fall into the category of supertasters, but I suspect that many HSPs can identify with this description.

Research conducted by Winnie Dunn also shows that people differ in their perception of sensory information. She mapped how people process sensory stimuli.[8] She distinguishes between a low and a high neurological threshold to perceive stimuli. She links a high threshold to habituation and a low threshold to sensitization. She also makes a distinction between the strategy of seeking out or avoiding stimuli. This is visualized in Figure 5.2.

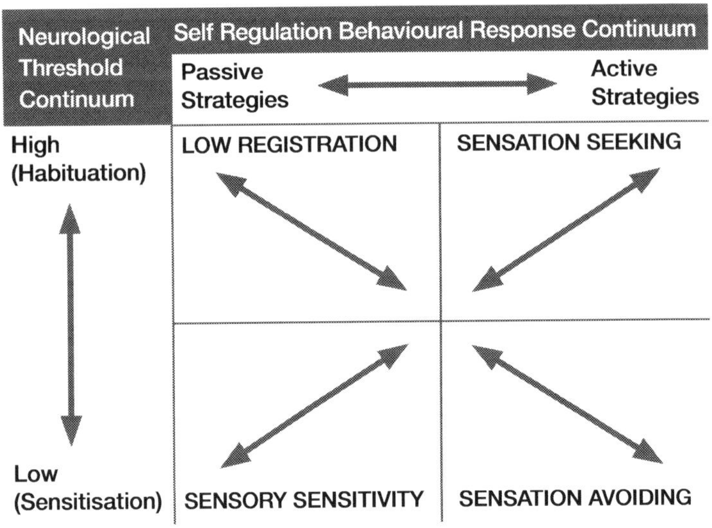

Figure 5.2 The four categories of Dunn (2007)

This creates four categories:

Low registration: These people receive stimuli (too) late. As a result, they sometimes miss information. They are passive in their strategy. They often need to be touched and addressed very directly in order to keep their attention.

Sensory sensitivity: Sensory sensitivity: These people perceive a lot and are easily overstimulated by this, which can make them irritable, demanding, or angry.

Sensation-seeking: These people register few stimuli, but seek them out in order to gain pleasure from experiencing them anyway. For example, they want to touch everything, or they constantly make noises during work or play.

Sensation avoiding: These people prefer to avoid stimuli to which they are sensitive. They experience a lot and regulate this by avoiding stimuli. For example, they stay away from busy parties, do not want to play in the sand, or refuse certain foods.

According to Dunn, it is possible to have different strategies for the different senses. You may take an avoiding approach when it comes to taste, while seeking out visual stimuli. You may not be able to tolerate sound, while motion sensations, such as rocking back and forth on the swings, are never too fast for you.
Highly sensitive people do not automatically belong to the category of sensory sensitivity, where much is perceived and a passive strategy is taken. Highly sensitive people can also adopt the strategy to avoid stimuli. And there are even highly sensitive people who seek out stimuli. It can be compared to Bartoshuk's supertasters. Some supertasters avoid foods with strong flavors, while other supertasters enjoy the strong kick the bitter gives them and eat a lot of bitter foods.

The terminology used by Dunn can cause confusion about what high sensitivity is. In her definition, people with strong sensory sensitivity are the people who notice a lot of stimuli and can become overstimulated by it. It is true that almost all highly sensitive people perceive strongly with at least one sense, and overstimulation is certainly not unfamiliar to them, but the definition of high sensitivity is broader than just sensory sensitivity. Intense processing of information is a core part of high sensitivity and Dunn does not mention this. Moreover, highly sensitive people differ in the way they deal with sensations. Therefore, highly sensitive people do not necessarily find themselves in the 'sensory sensitivity' category.

Back to Caitlin's dress. How can there be differences in perception? A survey of 1400 people shows that 57% see the actual blue-black color combination. The rest perceives something different: 30% sees white-gold, 11% sees blue-brown and 2% sees a different combination.[9] Women and the elderly in particular see gold and white. The researchers suspect that these differences are caused by the way the brain draws conclusions. If your brain concludes that a photo was taken with artificial light, it corrects the perception. Artificial light is often bluish and when we make that correction, we see bluish objects as white. Thus, the brain 'sees' a white-gold dress. People who subconsciously rely on daylight see blue-black.

Perception through the senses therefore differs between people. Apart from disorders, differences can exist due to genetic predisposition, the functioning of the brain, or processes such as habituation and sensitization.[10] It is still unclear how this works exactly, but highly sensitive people indicate they can perceive strongly with at least one sense. Sometimes this leads to an increased burden, but sometimes also to a greater enjoyment of sensations.

5.2 EMOTIONAL STIMULI

In that Italian restaurant at the beginning of Chapter 4, with one glance at my coworker I could feel how frustrated he was. I also understood perfectly where that frustration came from. He had been tasked with a new topic which he had no affinity with by the head of department. On top of that, he had to work with a colleague from another department who worked from a completely different angle. He felt quite misunderstood. And angry. One look at his face made my body tighten. It was as if his underlying anger had settled in my body. It bothered me, but I also sympathized with him.

At the same time, I recognized helplessness in the intern's gaze. I felt how he didn't know what to do. Even made himself small to escape the wrath of our colleague. I knew he was considering quitting his internship because he felt he wasn't of any use anyway. He had 'failed' before. That feeling of powerlessness took hold of me. It felt as if he almost slid over the edge into the chasm.

By the time dessert was served, my head had finally calmed down, the critical voices had faded into the background and my shoulders were more relaxed. I enjoyed the fun my table companions had together. I still had too little energy to participate in the conversation, but I could follow it. I saw my friend beaming as she talked about her dance classes. The new dance she had now almost mastered. I saw her standing on that dance floor in my mind's eye for a moment and felt her ecstasy. The feeling of being free from everything. Letting yourself be carried away by the music, gracefully following your body. The blissful feeling when your feet automatically do what they are supposed to do. Right on beat. She was only on that dance floor for a few seconds, but I floated along on her emotions.

We are social animals. Although we are no longer threatened by predators on a daily basis, we still need the social group to survive. It is therefore important for every person to be able to maintain social contacts. It is crucial to be able to estimate how others feel and what their intentions are. There are strong indications that HSPs perceive information about the emotional state of others more strongly.
Almost all highly sensitive people indicate through self-reporting that they are sensitive to the mood of others.[11] Sometimes it affects them so greatly that they suffer from that emotion all day long. They feel uncomfortable, cannot get to work properly, or avoid other people.

Mirror neurons can explain this aspect of high sensitivity. As I described in Chapter 3, mirror neurons are a relatively new discovery. When you see a person doing something, these neurons become similarly active as if you were doing it yourself. Watching a researcher pick up a raisin activates the same area as if you were picking up that raisin yourself. Seeing someone else cry activates the same areas as if you were crying yourself. Information is exchanged between two brains through an invisible connection: a so-called neural WiFi.[12]

In highly sensitive people, the brain areas with mirror neurons are activated more often and more strongly. These include the premotor area (PMA), the inferior parietal lobe (IPL), the insula, the temporo-parietal junction (TPJ) and the inferior frontal gyrus (IFG).[13] Research by Bianca Acevedo and colleagues (2014) shows that in certain situations, all these areas are more strongly activated in highly sensitive people. They asked 18 newlyweds to look at pictures of their partner and of a stranger while being in an fMRI scanner. The facial expressions in the photos were happy or sad. They were subsequently asked to indicate for a number of emotions to what extent – on a scale from 1 to 4 – the photo evoked these in them. To distinguish between highly sensitive and non-highly sensitive people, the respondents completed the HSP test.

After one year, 13 of them were examined again.[14] In the second round of research, the respondents were shown neutral facial expressions of their partner and a stranger in addition to happy and sad faces. As expected, all respondents experienced stronger emotions when they saw their partner than when they saw a stranger. Both positive and negative facial expressions of the partner evoked more intense emotions than comparable photos of a stranger. When compared to non-highly sensitive people, HSPs experienced even stronger emotions when it came to their partner's happy face. Furthermore, their brain was also more strongly activated while looking at the photos. Looking at pictures of a happy partner, a sad partner, or a happy stranger more strongly activated (among other things) areas of the brain where mirror neurons can be found. Specifically, the premotor area, the inferior frontal gyrus, and the insula.[15]

Other research by Bianca Acevedo also shows that the temporo-parietal junction (TPJ) is activated more often and more strongly in HSPs.[16] The TPJ is a brain area where many mirror neurons are located and is specifically involved in cognitive empathy (understanding the other person's situation). In Acevedo's research, this brain region appears to always be activated when processing emotional information, both with images of people and images of situations (section 7.2 takes a closer look at empathy).

Highly sensitive people are therefore wired to tune in to others, be it their own partner, or a stranger. Acevedo's (2014) results show that the activation is much stronger with their own partners. So a highly sensitive person tunes in strongly to others and intensely to their own partner in particular compared to the degree to which non-highly sensitive people tune in to others.
Although it is sometimes suggested that high sensitivity is mainly associated with negative emotions, the attention and responsiveness to positive emotions appears to be greater. In Acevedo's study, images of a sad stranger did not lead to more brain activation, but images of a happy stranger did.[17]
This is supported by Jagiellowicz's research (2012) where respondents looked at emotion-evoking photos.[18] Jadzia Jagiellowicz obtained her PhD by conducting research on the connection between sensory-processing sensitivity (high sensitivity) and emotional reactivity. She examined the response of 9 highly sensitive and 11 non-highly sensitive female college students to emotion-evoking photos. The photos were selected from the International Affective Picture System (IAPS, an international database containing emotional photos) and had a positive, negative or neutral meaning. For example, they showed cupcakes, smiling people, an umbrella, a fly on a cake, or polluted water. The students' brains were scanned while looking at the images. Afterwards, they indicated how strong the experienced emotion was and how much tension the image evoked in them.

The results showed that highly sensitive people experienced more intense emotions with positive images than non-highly sensitive people.[19] Jagiellowicz' article from 2016, in which she describes the same test, also shows that highly sensitive people experience an even stronger reaction to positive images than to negative ones. In both situations, their response was stronger compared to non-highly sensitive people, but the difference was greater with positive images.[20]

Meaning, highly sensitive people probably sympathize with the emotions of others because the areas of the brain containing mirror neurons are more strongly activated. Those mirror neurons work like a neural WiFi, causing emotions to be taken over. I felt the powerless feeling of that intern. But positive emotions can also be adopted. There are even indications that highly sensitive people are even more influenced by another person's positive emotions. I could therefore easily relate to that blissful feeling my friend experienced on the dance floor.

5.3 PERCEIVING DETAILS

What do you notice in your environment? Can you spot the smallest things or do you quickly overlook changes? The average person is change blind. Meaning you do not notice those changes you do not expect. That is why a new pair of glasses or a fresh haircut occasionally go unnoticed.
Highly sensitive people do notice those small changes. They are better able to see the smallest details. In the Italian restaurant, I noticed that the seating of the chair at the table on the left was somewhat splintered. Saw the table leg that would prevent a relaxed leg position. The speaker box directly above the seat. I could not see the seat of the chair at the table on the right, but I could still see the ribbon of the cushion tied to the seat. That is how I knew it would be a more comfortable chair. I also noticed the table legs were positioned differently, so these would not bother me. And I saw there was a heater nearby, so I would not get cold from the door to the kitchen that was constantly swinging open.

Jadzia Jagiellowicz and colleagues examined how this sharper perception of highly sensitive people works exactly.[21] In their 2011 study, 16 students were asked to look at 16 black-and-white photos in an fMRI scanner and point out the differences compared to the edited photo which was shown right after. These included photographs of meadows and houses (see figure 5.3). The students who participated completed the HSP scale in order to be able to establish differences between highly sensitive and non-highly sensitive people.

Pictures A and B in Figure 5.3 are the original pictures, to which major (C) and minor (D) changes have been made.

The response time and accuracy of detecting differences in the photos could be calculated for only 12 respondents. Within that group it

Figure 5.3 Pictures from Jagiellowicz's research (2011)

could not be established that highly sensitive people are more accurate in identifying differences. They did discover that highly sensitive people needed more time to detect small differences in a picture. During that process of detecting small differences, the visual focus areas appeared to be more strongly activated in highly sensitive people than in non-highly sensitive people.[22]

Research by Friederike Gerstenberg (2012) showed that HSPs process visual information faster and more accurately. In this study, 89 students indicated whether the letter T was visible in 120 pictures. Half of the pictures featured a T in a 90 or 270 degrees position. Between 4 and 20 distractors were added to the images in the shape of an L in four positions: 0, 90, 180 or 270 degrees. The students sat at a computer and were instructed to press A as soon as possible whenever a T was visible, and L if it was not.

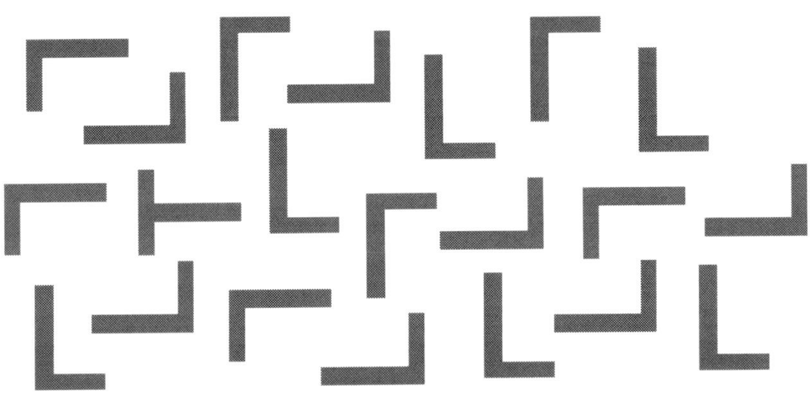

Figure 5.4 Example of a puzzle picture featuring a T surrounded by distractors

This research by Gerstenberg shows that highly sensitive people make significantly fewer mistakes during the task.[23] They thus appear to be better able to perceive subtle information accurately. Interestingly, they also respond significantly faster. This contradicts Jagiellowicz's research where highly sensitive people needed more time to notice differences. This may be the case because the images used in Jagiellowicz's research were more complicated. In any case, Gerstenberg's research demonstrates that highly sensitive people can process visual details faster and more accurately than non-highly sensitive people.

The same effect was found by Roiser and colleagues (2006). She examined whether people with different 5-HTTLPR variants score differently on tasks. There are three variants of the gene: s/s, s/l and l/l. Highly sensitive people are more likely to have the first variant. In the study, the participants completed many different tests, from attention-based tasks to decision-making games. One of the tests was similar to Gerstenberg's. Participants had to indicate whether they saw an R or an F in the usual manner or in mirrored. The symbol could be found in different positions, varying between 0 and 360 degrees (at intervals of 30 degrees). The people with an s/s variant performed this assignment much more accurately.[24] This result confirms Gerstenberg's finding that highly sensitive people score better on attention-based tasks than non-highly sensitive people.

In 2009, Borg and colleagues showed that people with the s/s genotype also score better on a task that measures both attention and cognitive flexibility.[25] They asked 54 Swedish men and women between the ages of 20 and 55 to take the so-called Wisconsin card sorting test (WCST) (see box). Borg concluded that people with the s/s variant made fewer mistakes and understood more quickly which categories they could create in order to sort the cards. He claims they can focus their attention better, and therefore respond better to visual information and feedback from the examiner, and scored better on problem solving.

Wisconsin card sorting test

This test is widely used to detect impairments in cognitive flexibility. In the WCST, the participant is presented with a mixed stack of cards (128 cards by default). Each card contains a variation of three possible attributes: color, number, and shape. Each attribute can have four varieties. For example the colors red, yellow, green, or blue, the numbers 1, 2, 3 or 4 and the shapes cross, triangle, circle, or star. The participant is instructed to sort the cards into four piles. During this process, the examiner tries to get the participant to change his sorting strategy by saying 'wrong'. The intention is for the participant to choose a new criterion. This says something about cognitive flexibility. The test ends when the competitor has correctly sorted a certain number of categories or when all cards are gone. The score is based on the number of errors and the number of categories the participant has created.

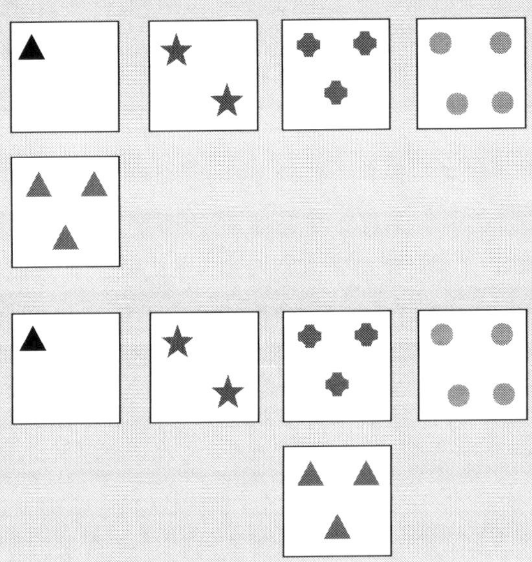

Figure 5.5 Example of two sorting strategies in the WCST.
Source: Wikipedia.nl, Albert Kok

The results of Gerstenberg's (2012) study of highly sensitive people are thus consistent with research among carriers of the s/s variant of the 5-HTTLPR gene: highly sensitive people focus their attention better and therefore respond more accurately to visual tasks.
Gerstenberg also asked her participants what their level of stress was before and after the detection task. Students who are highly sensitive experienced a stronger increase in stress. Better performance with regard to accuracy and speed therefore does cost something: it results in a greater feeling of stress. I will revisit this subject in Chapter 8.

5.4 SUMMARY

I now understand why a visit to a carnival demands so much energy from me. My ability to perceive is highly developed. Sounds, lights, and smells enter my senses intensely. It is as if they are all calling for my attention and my eyes are flickering back and forth to accommodate each and every stimulus.
On top of that, there are emotional stimuli. Even though I do not know the people I see at the carnival, their emotions can affect me. Not all of them, thankfully. But I do feel the emotions of people who find themselves in a situation I recognize, such as being on a scary ride, being in love, or having a lover's spat.
The observation of subtle details also contributes to overstimulation. The grabber in the claw machine that's just a little crooked, making winning impossible. The loose stitches on the teddy bear, leading your 'grand prize' to be ruined on day one. The cinnamon sticks that are definitely a little shorter at that one stand. My brain has to process all this information, and it does so in depth.

CHAPTER 6

Pause-to-check

When I first read about the pause-to-check system in a book by Elaine Aron, I suddenly understood why new playgrounds were always so frustrating for our family.

In the area, we lived when our kids were young, there were plenty of activities for children. As good parents, we wanted to take them to a different playground every weekend. We would pick a park and fill our bags with snacks and drinks. However, week after week, frustration would emerge upon arrival. Our children did not seem interested in all those fun activities. They just wanted to sit with us. We responded indignantly. Why wouldn't they play? Surely, we came here just for them. Then why didn't they enjoy it? Other children played happily, but our kids just sat there.

I can still see it. Two children who observed what was happening from their parents' laps or from behind their backs. Watched the playground and the other children. Two parents who encouraged them to play. Pointed out the slide and the swings. Drew their attention to the fun others were having. Encouraged them to walk over there. Only after half an hour, when we were about to give up and go home again, did my children take some cautious steps towards the play equipment.

Later I understood that their observation period is important to them. Think first, then act. First check how high the slide is. How wide the steps of the stairs are. Whether there is a puddle at the end. And how busy the children playing there are. Once that information has been processed, the child knows what he or she should take into account and then can participate in the situation. Stimulating or even pushing the child in that phase is counterproductive. Even more stimuli will then come in, and overstimulation is just around the corner.
We discovered that a familiar playground required much less observation time. After all, much of the information had already been processed before. In a familiar playground, they enjoyed themselves more, they played more freely. And they felt safe enough to push their boundaries. We no longer went to a new place every weekend, but happily visited our trusted old playground in the neighborhood. We alternated with something new every now and then to teach them how to deal with new circumstances. The weekends became a lot more relaxed for all of us.

In the previous chapter I wrote that highly sensitive people perceive more. In this chapter I describe what happens when everything that has been perceived is processed.
High sensitivity is a trait where information is processed before taking action. This system, which is the main theme of this chapter, is also called the pause-to-check system. This consists of placing information in the bigger picture (section 6.2) and sensory integration (section 6.3).

6.1 BEHAVIOR INHIBITING SYSTEM

A child who observes before participating shows so-called 'inhibited behavior'. Jerome Kagan, who researched the response of babies to a mobile spoke of inhibited and uninhibited children.[1] This inhibited behavior was often approached by researchers as deviant behavior. However, in the early 1980s, Gray already described the evolutionary

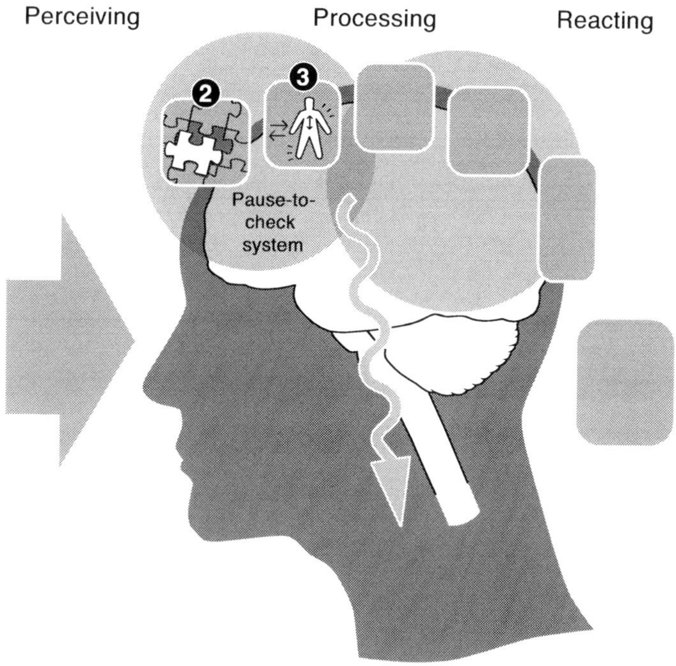

Figure 6.1 The highly sensitive brain: pause-to-check system

function of inhibited behavior. He introduced the concepts behavioral inhibition system (BIS) and behavioral activation system (BAS). In 2000, he completed this theory.[2]

According to him, the BIS produces alert attention and a pause in activity so that conflicting information can be processed. The BAS is aimed at fulfilling needs and the urge to go for something. In the playground situation, children with a strong BIS will therefore first observe before climbing on the slide. Children with a strong BAS immediately want to experience that wonderful feeling of going down the slide and are on the slide before you know it.

When a threat occurs, according to Gray, a third system comes into operation: fight, flight, or freeze.[3] He therefore distinguishes between inhibited behavior and a stress response. Gray's research has brought more attention to the benefit of inhibited behavior.

In previous studies, inhibited behavior was linked to a stronger experience of stress and anxiety. Bar-Haim and colleagues (2009) show, however, that inhibited adolescents react more strongly to all situations. In both threatening and rewarding situations, they take time to assess the situation and their response is stronger compared to uninhibited people. Inhibited behavior does not necessarily mean that the person experiences anxiety. It is a strategy of alert attention, in order to process all relevant information before taking action.

Elaine Aron uses the hypothesis that this BIS is the foundation of high sensitivity.[4] Highly sensitive people have a strong behavior-inhibiting system. They take a pause to process information. This does not mean that highly sensitive people are inhibited at all times. They are particularly so in new situations or in situations where interests have suddenly changed.[5]
Some highly sensitive people also have strong behavioral activation systems. They do not seem at all restrained in their behavior. They like to get into new situations and appear adventurous to the outside world. This group of highly sensitive people has both systems. They take action quickly, but also analyze the information from the environment in the few seconds before participating. Unlike people who only have a strong BAS, they rarely cause mishaps and make fewer mistakes. This group is often referred to as the HSP/HSS. HSS stands for high sensation seeker.[6]

An indication that the BIS is indeed the underlying mechanism in high sensitivity comes from research by Bianca Acevedo in which newlyweds looked at portrait photos. Results showed that the premotor area was always strongly activated in highly sensitive people. This premotor area is involved in unconscious control of behavior and action planning, and stronger activation of this area may indicate a strong BIS presence.[7]
Research by Homberg and colleagues on 5-HTTLPR also links the s/s variant, which is more common in highly sensitive people, to the BIS.[8]

Brain studies show that highly sensitive people – when compared to non-highly sensitive people – use more brain areas at the same time when performing a task. This is another indication that highly sensitive people process information in depth.[9] These studies tell us that the information is processed with many more areas of the brain, thus indicating more different analysis operations taking place and a greater connectivity within the brain.
This is supported by the stronger activation of the default mode network (DMN). This DMN is more active in highly sensitive people in all emotional tasks, but also in processing non-emotional information.[10] This DMN is, as can be read in chapter 3, an area that is active when no task has to be performed and the brain 'wanders', think of recalling memories or putting yourself in another person's shoes. In highly sensitive people, this area therefore remains active during the processing of information. This may mean that information is analyzed on different levels at the same time.

6.2 THE BIGGER PICTURE

During the processing and analysis of information, the brain of highly sensitive people connects with what is already known from previous experiences. As long as sufficient meaning cannot be given to the incoming information, the brain continues to search. This is visible in highly sensitive children when they do not understand the purpose of an assignment. Too little tools are available to understand what the new information means. Without those tools they cannot start the assignments. They freeze – sit and stare – or ask questions until the context is clear to them.[11] This way of thinking also causes them to make connections others do not see. They see patterns which can surprise you as an adult. This explains why many parents indicate that their highly sensitive child has wise insights.[12]

Research by Art Aron, Elaine Aron's husband, and colleagues sheds light on this.[13] They asked 20 subjects, 10 Americans and 10 Asians, to conduct several exercises while their brains were being scanned. The subjects had to compare the absolute and the relative length of lines (see Figure 6.2). When assessing relative length, you need to consider context. In this case, a square enclosing the line. If the line in the large square is relatively the same length as in the small square, it is considered a match. The relative task turned out to be easier for Asians. This could be seen from the intensity of their brain activity.[14]

When assessing the absolute length, the question is whether the line segments are exactly the same length. You should ignore the context (the square) and only look at the actual length of the line (see figure 6.2). The absolute comparison turned out to be easier for Americans. This study shows that a person's cultural background has an effect on the ease with which problems are solved. The American, individualistic culture makes tasks where the context does not have to be taken into account easier for Americans. In Asian culture, taking context into account is more self-evident, making the relative tasks easier for Asians.

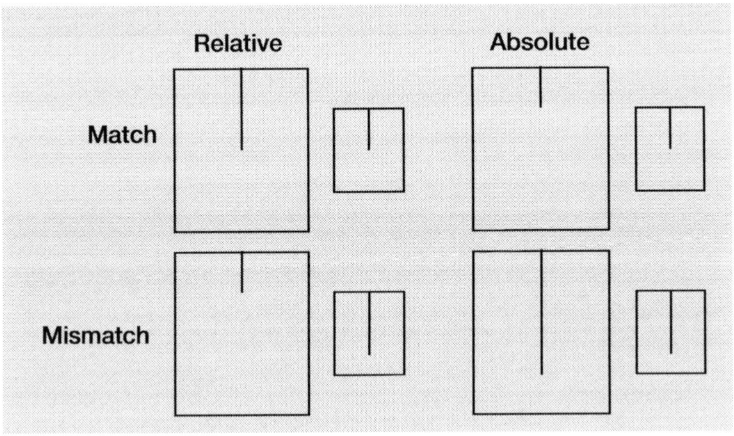

Figure 6.2 Relative and absolute length of lines (Aron, 2010)

When determining the relative length (left in figure 6.2), the square enclosing the line must be considered. The top image shows a match and the bottom image shows a mismatch. On the contrary, when determining the absolute length, the square must be disregarded. The top (right) image shows two equal line segments. In the bottom (right) image the lengths differ, resulting in a mismatch.

Solving a problem that is not easy for you is associated with higher brain activation. That difference was clearly visible. Americans showed more brain activation when solving relative problems and Asians with absolute problems. However, this was only the case for non-highly sensitive respondents. For highly sensitive participants, whether American or Asian, no difference was found: the relative and the absolute comparison cost an equal amount of effort.
In non-highly sensitive Americans and Asians, a large difference can be seen with regard to brain activity: the 'non-culture-specific' tasks require much more effort. It is as if their brain suddenly wakes up and has to work hard. However, highly sensitive Americans and Asians scored the same on both assignments. Non-culturally-specific assignments are thus no more difficult for highly sensitive people. This is because highly sensitive people process all stimuli in depth: they always get out their entire toolbox, whether the situation is 'normal' or 'different' – while the average person chooses a hammer or a saw in case of a problem and only uses the entire toolbox if they do not succeed with merely a hammer or saw.

6.3 SENSORY INTEGRATION

The brain is not separated from the body. It steers bodily processes and receives information from the body. The sense that perceives that information from the body is called interoception.[15] Although this sense is relatively unknown, Sherrington introduced this term as early as 1906. The sense of interoception signals where deficiencies or surpluses are present in the body. In this way, it detects whether you are thirsty or hungry, whether you need to go to the bathroom, or take a deep breath. Interoception is referred to as the eighth sense. After the five most famous senses – sight, hearing, smell, taste, and touch – balance and proprioception (awareness of the position of your body) are listed as sixth and seventh, and interoception as eighth.[16]

One person experiences interoceptive signals strongly and others barely do so. In the latter case, for example, a child notices too late that he or she needs to go to the bathroom, or someone does not detect that he is becoming dehydrated and needs to drink. Insensitivity to interoceptive signals can lead to problems such as chronic pain and anxiety, eating and sexual disorders. In addition, interoception is connected to, among other things, emotion regulation, empathy, (self) awareness, and decision-making.[17]

The most important area of the brain with regard to interoception is the insula. The insula registers all kinds of information from different parts of the body and exchanges information with the amygdala, hypothalamus, anterior cingulate cortex (ACC), orbitofrontal cortex (OFC), and dorsolateral prefrontal cortex (DLPFC).[18] What the entire highly sensitive brain does – the in-depth processing of information – the insula does in miniature. It connects signals from different sources. In this way, not only a physiological, but also a psychological balance is ensured.

The insula is more strongly activated in highly sensitive people than in non-highly sensitive people, especially with positive emotions and especially if the person had a good childhood.[19] The brain areas with which the insula exchanges information are also more strongly activated in HSPs. For example, the hypothalamus is more strongly activated when highly sensitive people process emotional information, be it positive or negative images.[20] The DLPFC appears to be activated more strongly when highly sensitive people look at their partner.[21]

The amygdala is only more strongly activated in HSPs who had a good childhood when they look at negative images.[22] Finally, the ACC is also more strongly activated in the processing of emotional information[23], although Acevedo's research seems to indicate that this is especially true for positive images.[24]

What can we conclude from this? First of all, we do not yet know whether highly sensitive people perceive interoceptive signals more strongly and/or more accurately. This kind of research is complicated anyway. Whether you are able to observe your own heart rate is often considered as an indication, but it is questionable whether this says anything about all other signals.[25] Besides, high sensitivity was not taken into account in these studies. Furthermore, a lack of concepts can leave the interoceptive signals unused. You may well register the signals, but if you do not know what meaning to give them, it is less useful. In addition to being able to perceive, the ability to interpret is therefore an important point.

Second, there seems to be an important distinction between positive and negative emotions and between HSPs who had a good childhood and HSPs who had a bad childhood. Positive emotions activate the insula, hypothalamus, dorsolateral prefrontal cortex, and anterior cingulate cortex more strongly in highly sensitive people than in non-highly sensitive people. This could mean they are better able to tune in to their own bodily signals with positive emotions. They experience what the situation does to them and activate the correct bodily processes. This could explain why highly sensitive people can enjoy the happiness of others, and probably especially that of their loved ones. Highly sensitive people who had a good childhood seem to be able to do this even better. For them, the insula is activated even more. In Chapter 8, I further discuss the difference between highly sensitive people who had a good and a bad childhood.

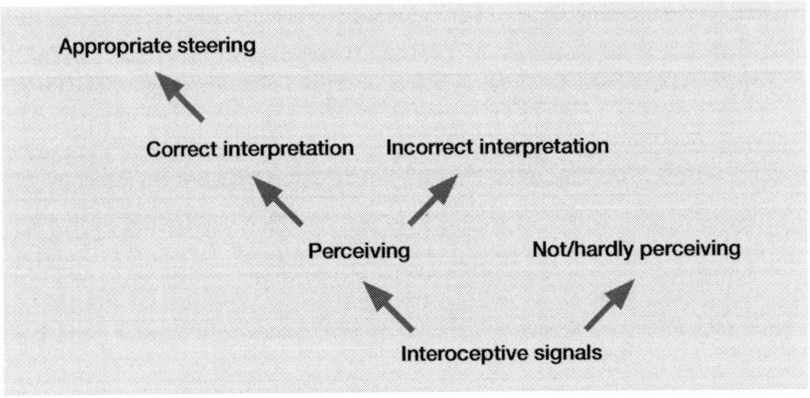

Figure 6.3 Perceiving interoceptive signals

We sometimes experience the signals from our body as a gut feeling. Your body sends out a signal which you cannot immediately explain rationally. Holzer (2017) links gut feelings and interoception. Gut feelings often do not enter our consciousness, but they do influence our emotions, beliefs, and decision-making. Barnaby Dunn's research shows that the degree of accuracy in interoception (in this case being able to correctly perceive your own heartbeat) influences intuitive decision-making.[26] Being able to perceive your internal signals better leads to better intuitive decisions. In addition, these people are more inclined to do something good for someone else; better interoception predicts a higher altruism score.[27] As such, Wager calls the insula an important link between cognition and feeling.[28]

The insula exchanges information with the hypothalamus. The hypothalamus activates the stress system and regulates important bodily functions. When the body detects stress, the hypothalamus triggers the production of stress hormones such as cortisol and (nor)adrenaline.[29] This will be elaborated further in chapter 9. In addition, the hypothalamus regulates your body temperature, hunger, thirst, sexual behavior, and aggression. Hence, it prepares the body for necessary action in various ways.

Research by Acevedo shows that in highly sensitive people the hypothalamus is always more strongly activated with incoming sensory information than in non-highly sensitive people, whether it concerns positive or negative information.[30] So they probably adjust their internal body processes to the situation more than others do.
The hypothalamus also has a strong connection with the hippocampus, the place where experiences are processed into memories and may or may not end up in the memory. The hippocampus is also more strongly activated in HSPs. This may indicate that highly sensitive people deeply process and store the effects stimuli have on them for future reference. In this way, they are more quickly prepared for future situations.[31]

6.4 SUMMARY

When I had to choose between the two seats in that Italian restaurant, I perceived several interoceptive signals. First of all, hunger. It was already later than I would usually have dinner and hunger has a strong effect on my mood. Elaine Aron describes this nicely with the term hangry: angry because you are hungry. Second, I noticed my shoulders tighten. The intention to sit next to my frustrated colleague immediately led to a feeling of stress and the accompanying physical manifestations. My shoulders always tighten and my breathing becomes shallower. At the time I did not notice the latter, but over the years I have come to recognize signals like this earlier.
Those seconds I used to think about the best place to sit are a good illustration of the pause-to-check system. I observed the situation first, before making a decision. I processed the information I registered in depth; all kinds of considerations went through my mind – and they had an effect on my body. In the next chapter I will go further into this depth of processing, in particular with regard to the content of the considerations: the optimal-option-ambition.

CHAPTER 7

Optimal-option-ambition

'Esther, can I talk to you for a moment?' From the look on my boss's face I can see that it's good news. Even before the door to his office is closed, he stumbles over his words in his enthusiasm and shares the good news. 'The board finally agreed. We will receive a major amount of money to finally start project Z. You have to do it, Esther. I can already picture it...'

My heart skips a beat. This is great. Project Z can be launched. This will allow our department to make a real impact. It would be wonderful to dive into this new topic, to draw up a tight project plan and get started with a team.

'You can pick whoever you want for your team,' I hear my boss say.

Up until now, I haven't answered. There is little opportunity for that due to his outpour. Who will I choose for this project? I prefer not to work in teams that are too big. I immediately have a few people in mind. They will have to be excused from other projects, but that won't be a problem. Although... One of those projects is assigned to my colleague. I'll call her Anne here. Her project is in the process of being finalized and she will certainly not appreciate it if people from her team no longer have time for the final phase. In addition, she will

be disappointed to say the least, if she doesn't get the new project. Her only project is almost finished. I still have two projects running.
'You'll say yes to this amazing opportunity, right?' My boss asks me. 'You are the right person for the job.'
I truly want nothing more than to lead this project. It was originally my idea and I know I can bring it to a successful conclusion. But is it the right decision? Anne is well-liked, sociable, and energetic. If the division of projects is seen as unfair, it will also affect the atmosphere in the department. We run large projects and have fun together. But when injustice is experienced, the work feels too hard. Of course, my colleagues are also happy for me to get the project. But there would be more dissatisfaction. Perhaps opposing groups could even arise. And that would certainly jeopardize the completion of current projects and thus the continued existence of the department. This became all too clear from the previous board meeting: they want to see results. I know which choice to make.
'This really seems like a project for Anne,' I answer. 'She has the right qualities for this. Ask her first if she would like to lead the project.'
I can see the surprise on his face. My boss was not prepared for that answer.

In this chapter I discuss the optimal-option-ambition: the automatic tendency of highly sensitive people to take the interests of others and the group as a whole into account. This is the second key component of information processing. The first (the pause-to-check system) was discussed in the previous chapter. There we read how highly sensitive people think before they act and how they have a stronger connection between brain and bodily processes than non-highly sensitive people. This chapter focuses on the question of what they specifically consider before they act. Which elements are included in the contemplation? The following elements are illustrated in figure 7.1 and discussed in this chapter: Analyzing the risks and opportunities (section 7.1), taking the social context into account (section 7.2), and formulating an action (section 7.3).

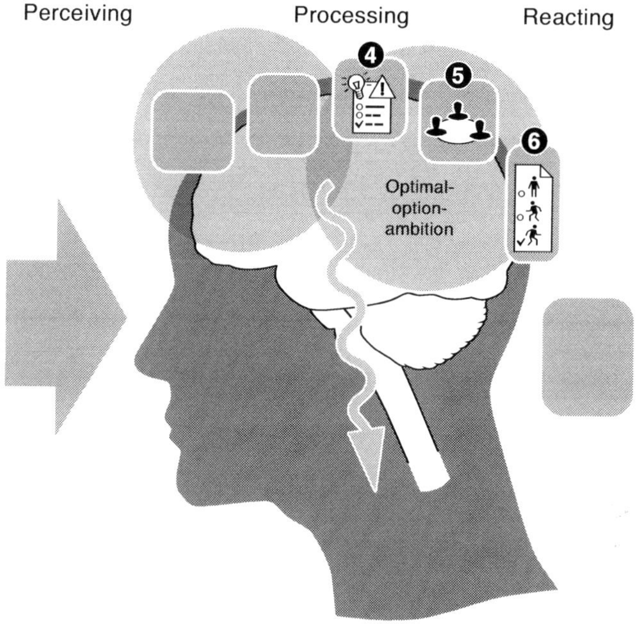

Figure 7.1 The highly sensitive brain: optimal-option-ambition

7.1 ANALYSIS OF RISKS AND CHANCES

Perceiving information seems to lead to a stream of associations in a highly sensitive person: he sees the potential risks, but certainly also the opportunities the situation entails. When my boss asked me to lead project Z, I did not immediately accept, even though this project had been my idea. I thought it would be a lot of fun to do and I thought I could bring it to a successful conclusion. My associations tumbled over each other. I saw great opportunities with this project. How we could tackle it, how it could contribute to the personal development of employees, but also how the report could ultimately make a real difference. I also saw risks. Which team members should not be put together. What effect it would have if I had to excuse people from other projects. What could happen on the social side of things. And how that could subsequently influence the progress of other projects.

When a highly sensitive employee shares his analysis of opportunities and risks with the group, the opportunities are received enthusiastically, the comments on risks are often less well-received. For the project group members, the highly sensitive colleague is considered to be someone who 'sees obstacles', who 'acts difficult' and 'is negative'. The comment is dismissed or sometimes even ignored. These employees 'will see how it goes' and think 'all in good time'. Obviously, these differences lead to friction. Highly sensitive employees like to arrange things well in advance and, according to them, the 'we'll-see-how-it-goes' attitude shows little sense of responsibility. Speed often takes precedence. The project is simply launched. Sometimes it runs like a charm and other times those identified risks do indeed jeopardize its progress. But at that point, there is very little that can be done.

Assessing risks

No research has been conducted yet into the difference between highly sensitive and non-highly sensitive people with regard to the assessment of risks. However, Qinghua He and his colleagues did conduct research in 2010 that may shed some light on this matter. They study the effect of the presence of a particular gene on decision-making under ambiguity and risk (see box). They studied the gene 5-HTTLPR, which, as I described in Chapter 1, is associated with high sensitivity.
572 students from Beijing Normal University took part in the study.[1] By means of a blood test it was determined which 5-HTTLPR variant they had: two short alleles (s/s), two long alleles (l/l) or a combination (s/l). In addition, participants completed an intelligence test and took part in two computerized decision-making tests, the Iowa Gambling Task (IGT) and the Loss Aversion Task (LAT). See the box for a description of these two tests.

The Iowa Gambling Task (IGT)

This task is used to understand how people make choices when not all information is known to them. This is called decision-making under ambiguity (a situation open to several explanations). It was developed by researchers at the University of Iowa.[2] Participants may choose cards from four different decks on the computer. Each card yields an amount of profit or loss. Two decks deliver high initial wins, but long-term losses (the bad decks). The other two decks have lower wins on the first cards, but bigger wins in the long run (the good decks). In He's experiment, this entailed a 250 yuan loss if you drew ten cards from the bad decks, against a 250 yuan profit if you took ten cards from a good deck. The purpose of the assignment is to yield the highest possible profit. In time, the participants should figure out the division of cards into good and bad decks and mainly choose cards from the right deck. However, there appear to be many differences with regard to the amount of profit people yield in this test.

The Loss Aversion Task (LAT)

This is also a psychological task to simulate decision making. Here, the participants were asked if they wanted to take a gamble, where the possible profit (ranging between 10 and 40 yuan) and the loss (between 5 and 20 yuan) were shown.
For example: 'Do you want to take this gamble? If you lose, you lose 15 yuan, if you win, you receive 20 yuan.' The participant may say yes or no to this bet. A coin determines whether he wins or loses. Nothing happens if he refuses to take the gamble. The assignment is to gain as much money as possible.

This study showed that men with one or two l alleles earned more during the IGT. 100 rounds of this game were played and after about 20 rounds, the participants learned that the deck which appeared to have higher winnings led to a loss in the long run. After that point, there were no significant differences between people with two s alleles and one or two l alleles. Only in the uncertain, ambiguous period when the results of the decks are not yet clear, do the s participants score lower. The s participants probably avoided the decks which yielded the initial loss.
We might be looking at a difference between the sexes, however. Van den Bos, Homberg and Visser (2013) show in their review that, during the IGT, men take longer-term profit into account, more so than women do. According to these researchers, the differences between people with an s/s variant and those with an l allele are explained by differences in gender and brain volume (specifically the orbitofrontal cortex). Therefore, the influence of the 5-HTTLPR gene on the results of the IGT is still unclear.

With the LAT, participants in He's study were allowed to decide whether to take a gamble or not. They were told how high the possible profit and possible loss was. About 55% of the bets offered were accepted by the participants. Typically, they would bet if the win was at least twice the loss. Respondents with two s alleles responded differently. In case of big losses, they refused the bet, even though the possible profit was twice as big. He and colleagues conclude that they have a greater loss aversion. Loss aversion is the phenomenon where people are more aware of the possibility of losing money or things than of the possibility of gaining them. However, you could also argue that not gambling a loss of 20 yuan, even though there is a possible profit of 40 yuan, means you are being cautious. As the participants were given the goal to gain as much money as possible.

Although the study was not specifically conducted in highly sensitive people, the link between high sensitivity and the s/s variant of 5-HTTLPR suggests that highly sensitive people generally avoid high risks more often than non-highly sensitive people.

Decision making in the brain

One brain area important in decision making is the dorsolateral prefrontal cortex (DLPFC). The DLPFC regulates higher-order cognitive processes such as decision-making, complex tasks, and executive functions. An interesting study by Knoch and colleagues (2006), in which participants played a decision-making game, showed that this brain area becomes active when someone decides whether or not to perform a certain action.[3] The brain area is mainly active in actions that are perceived as fair and less in selfish actions.[4]

Bianca Acevedo's research where newlyweds looked at portrait pictures shows that the DLPFC is more activated in highly sensitive people than in non-highly sensitive people when they look at their partner.[5] This may indicate that highly sensitive people are more strongly activated to do something, especially something beneficial to others. This applies to both the sad as well as to the happy face of their partner. The facial expression of the partner thus not only activates emotions (via the mirror neurons as we saw in section 5.2) but also activates fair action.

Thus, highly sensitive people are probably more focused on the risks when making a decision than non-highly sensitive people. We can conclude this from He's research, which shows that people with the s/s genotype of the 5-HTTLPR gene are risk-averse.[6] This is supported by research showing that brain areas involved in decision-making are more strongly activated when processing emotional information in HSPs than in non-highly sensitive people. However, more research is needed regarding the difference between highly sensitive and non-highly sensitive people when it comes to estimating risks and opportunities and making decisions.

7.2 TAKING THE SOCIAL CONTEXT INTO ACCOUNT

Highly sensitive people have a lot of consideration for their immediate environment. The interests of others play a major role in the processing of information and in reaching a decision. As illustrated in the previous section, in my considerations whether or not to lead project Z, many different opportunities and risks crossed my mind. With regard to planning as well as financial, personal, and social aspects. At first, I was thrilled when my boss told me the funding for project Z had finally come through. Preferably, I would have started straight away. My brain was already creating all kinds of images of how I would do it.

But even in those visions of the future I also scanned the social context. What were the interests of my colleagues? How would they react to the new situation? And where could that lead us? If they perceived it to be unfair that not Anne but I would lead the new project, what would the atmosphere be like? What would that mean for mutual cooperation? Which colleagues would be affected? How would that affect the progress of the project? Even though, the question was what *I* wanted, my brain also mapped the consequences for social interaction and the effects it would have on my colleagues. Those consequences outweighed my own interests in making my decision. Only years later did I discover that I very frequently subordinated my own interests to the interests of the group. It was an automatic process which I can now consciously bring to a halt.

Everyone takes the social context into account, because, as humans, we depend on the group for our survival – although this feeling appears to be diminishing in individualistic societies. Brain research has shown, however, that highly sensitive people make these considerations more often and more intensively. It even seems to be an automatic response of the highly sensitive brain: in every situation, attention is paid to how one's own reactions will be received in the social context. In this context, I further explain four brain areas: the anterior cingulate cortex, the medial prefrontal cortex, the insula, and the areas with mirror neurons (inferior frontal gyrus and temporo-parietal junction).

Anterior cingulate cortex

First of all, the consideration for the social context is illustrated by the stronger activation of the anterior cingulate cortex (ACC). The ACC is located in the cingulate cortex, which is part of the limbic system. The ACC can be characterized as an error radar. It is active with cognitive errors, for example when contradictory tasks have to be performed, such as with the Stroop test. Where the participants must state the colors of the words, while the words themselves also describe colors. For example, the word 'green' is printed in blue letters, and the participant must then say 'blue'.[7]

What is important in this context is the ACC as a social error radar. The ACC assesses whether its own responses are socially rewarded or punished. The ACC gives, as it were, an alarm signal if errors are likely to occur in relation to others.[8] For example, it is highly active when you feel left out.

As mentioned, in 2012 Jadzia Jagiellowicz examined the brain responses of highly sensitive people to emotion-evoking photos. She studied 9 highly sensitive and 11 non-highly sensitive students.[9] The students' brains were scanned while looking at the photos. Subsequently, they indicated how strong the emotions they experienced were and how much tension the image evoked in them. These emotional photos activated the ACC of highly sensitive people more strongly. In particular, the ventral region, which happens to be the location of the social error radar.[10]

The 2017 study by Bianca Acevedo with a similar design (14 students looked at emotional images in an fMRI scan) showed the same results. There too, the ACC was more strongly activated in highly sensitive people.[11] When emotion is evoked (by a photo of a person or a situation), this seems to strongly activate the social error radar in highly sensitive people. They establish a link between the information and the consequences for (their position in) the group.

The connection between the ACC and social exclusion has been examined using the so-called cyberball game (see box).[12] In this video game people throw a ball around. The game is programmed in such a way that, after a while, the participant no longer gets the ball. This increases the subjective level of stress. The more stress people experience from this, the more strongly their ACC is activated.[13] The ACC is thus involved in comparing yourself with others and, among other things, becomes more strongly activated when you feel excluded. Another area heavily involved in this process, the insula, will be discussed below.[14]

Cyberball game

The cyberball game is derived from the ball toss experiment developed by Kip Williams and his colleagues at Purdue University.[15] Three people take turns throwing the ball to each other. Two of the three are part of the experiment without the third participant being aware of this. After some time they only throw the ball at each other. The third participant, the test subject, is excluded and asked about his emotions after the experiment. The emotions turn out to be universal; everyone feels left out. Even people with a high degree of self-esteem experience negative feelings after this game.

In the cyberball variant, the ball is thrown around via a computer. In this situation, too, two participants are part of the experiment (or these roles are played by a computer) without the third knowing. In the first minutes, he gets the ball just as often as the others, in the last minutes he does not get the ball at all. Exclusion in the cyberball game also evokes strong negative emotions in everyone, even when the participants know their fellow players are computers.[16] Even when exclusion is financially rewarded and continuing to participate in the game costs money, the experience of being excluded still hurts a lot.[17]

The ACC is also responsible for the physical regulation of, for example, the bodily responses to emotional stimuli, such as changes in heart rate and blood pressure. This could mean that highly sensitive people are also more likely to experience physical effects from problems they perceive in social situations. In other words: the highly sensitive brain assesses the consequences for social situations and the body is partly influenced by this.

It is striking that sensitivity to pain – which we discussed in section 5.1 – appears to be related to the sensitivity to social exclusion. In a study using the same cyberball game, it was shown that people with a low pain threshold report more negative feelings when they are excluded than people with a higher pain threshold.[18]

Medial prefrontal cortex

A second brain region important in taking the social context into account is the medial prefrontal cortex (mPFC). This cerebral lobe is an important part of the social brain and helps us think about ourselves in relation to the other. The anterior cingulate cortex is located right next to this brain area. Both the ACC and the mPFC are more strongly activated with all emotional photos, but the mPFC shows some differences between positive and negative images.

In 2017, Acevedo and her colleagues asked 14 female college students to look at pictures while they were in an fMRI scanner.[19] The participants completed the HSP scale and questionnaires about the quality of their upbringing (see also box in section 8.3). In the scanner they looked at six blocks of four photos. These photos each had a positive, negative, or neutral emotional charge. These photos were selected from a database of emotion-evoking photos (IAPS). Subsequently, the students had to indicate how high their tension level was on a scale from 1 to 7. This study showed a stronger activation of the mPFC in highly sensitive people.[20] More specifically: with negative photos, subareas of the mPFC become more activated than in non-highly sensitive people.
Three areas can be distinguished. The upper part (the dorsal medial PFC) links value to action. It evaluates the actions of others and how you relate to others. Think about how you judge other people's posts on social media and how this makes you feel. This area is only activated more strongly in highly sensitive people who had a good childhood who experience negative emotions. The ventral area (vmPFC) is involved in assessing your own situation.[21] For example, when determining whether something also applies to you when you read the examples in this book. In addition, this area has been linked to social behavior in various studies; ranging from donating money to being nice to someone who is being left out.[22] When compared to non-highly sensitive people, this area appears to be more strongly activated in all highly sensitive people when they look at negative images.[23]

For highly sensitive people, especially negative images result in making comparisons between themselves and others. Perhaps they regulate the strongly experienced emotions with the social brain's point of view; how we position ourselves in relation to the other also nuances our own experienced emotions. Kirsten Neff, for example, mentions common humanity, the realization that you are not the only one experiencing difficult moments, as one of the three aspects of self-compassion.[24] Research shows that the medial prefrontal cortex plays a large role in experiencing this aspect of self-compassion.[25] The fact that the medial prefrontal cortex is more strongly activated in highly sensitive people in situations where negative emotions are triggered, may indicate that they are not focused solely on their own negative experience. They connect it to the experiences of others and may take solace in it, or at least be aware that they are not alone in this experience.

The lowest area in the medial prefrontal cortex is the orbital mPFC. This area links value to outcomes. It plays a part in contemplating whether a response will turn out to be positive or negative for you. This area is just as strongly activated in highly sensitive people as in non-highly sensitive people.

Insula

The insula appears to be more strongly activated in highly sensitive people when they experience positive emotions.[26] The insula aligns interoceptive, affective, and emotional signals. In 6.3 I highlighted the importance of this brain area for the sense of interoception. It perceives signals from the body and interprets these in order to be able to exercise more control over other areas. The insula is also an important area when it comes to self-other perception (how you relate to others) and emotional awareness.[27] This brain area is more strongly activated in all highly sensitive people when they are shown images with positive emotions. This may mean that HSPs harmonize a lot within themselves (their bodily processes) as well as towards others. The anterior cingulate cortex and the medial prefrontal cortex also facilitate the self-other perception. This confirms that the highly sensitive brain is strongly focused on threats to the social connection within the group. In addition, the insula is involved in empathic processes, such as feeling others' pain (in cooperation with the ACC) or seeing things from others' perspectives (in cooperation with the mirror neurons).

Mirror neurons

The last 'social' area of the brain that is more strongly activated in highly sensitive people is the mirror neurons area, specifically the inferior frontal gyrus and the temporo-parietal junction. These, like the insula, are central to empathy.
In the inferior frontal gyrus (IFG) many mirror neurons are present. These neurons make it possible to experience what the other is experiencing. This mechanism is also discussed in section 5.2, regarding the perception of emotional stimuli. Highly sensitive people are very capable of perceiving information regarding the emotional state of the other. This is also relevant for information processing. The mirror neurons provide information about the mood of the other, which gives the social check more color.

The temporo-parietal junction (TPJ) is an important area for so-called mentalizing.[28] This process is also called theory of mind and means that you can understand someone else's position. It entails the cognitive side of empathy.
Simon Baron-Cohen distinguishes between two types of empathy: affective empathy (feeling another person's emotions) and cognitive empathy (being able to put yourself in another person's shoes with regard to perception).[29] The TPJ is linked to cognitive empathy.[30]

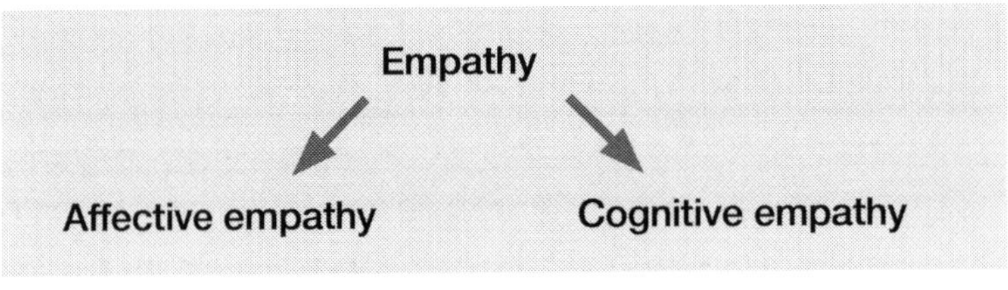

Figure 7.2 Two kinds of empathy

Cognitive empathy has a regulatory effect. Woodruff and Stevens indicate that your thoughts regarding the situation (cognitive empathy) can influence the emotion felt (affective empathy).[31] When you see someone stumble, it triggers different emotions in you. Strong emotions (affective empathy), however, often diminish when you consider the other person to be responsible (cognitive empathy) for the stumbling.

Sally-Anne-test

The Sally-Anne test is a neuropsychological experiment designed by Wimmer and Perner (1983) to test a person's ability to relate to the other.

The child watches a kind of puppet play performed by the researcher: 'One doll is called Sally, the other's name is Anne. Sally has a basket and a marble. Anne has a box. Sally puts the marble in her basket and covers it with a cloth. Then she walks out. Naughty Anne then secretly takes the marble and puts it in the box. Then Sally comes back. She would like to play with her marble.' The examiner then asks the child, 'Where will Sally look for her marble?' Or 'Where does Sally think her marble is?'

If the child is able to put himself in Sally's position, he will say, 'In the basket.' That is where Sally left the marble. Children who are not good at this, point to the place where the marble actually lies. A small portion of the four-year-old children provide the correct answer. Nearly all six-year-olds did. However, children with autism do not score very well on this.[32]

Highly sensitive people are expected to score high on such tests, because the activation of the temporo-parietal junction shows us that HSPs can relate to the other well. This ability to project oneself into the other is called theory of mind.

Research by Acevedo shows that, in certain situations, the inferior frontal gyrus and the temporo-parietal junction are more strongly activated in highly sensitive people.[33] The IFG is especially more strongly activated when highly sensitive people look at positive facial expressions.[34] With negative facial expressions, no stronger activation was found. This can mean that highly sensitive people mainly tune in to the other person's emotions if these are positive. Follow-up research showed that images with negative emotions even decreased activation in this area – as if HSPs were closing off the negative emotions.[35] This was especially true for highly sensitive people who experienced a bad childhood.

The TPJ is always more strongly activated in highly sensitive people when processing emotional images (of things and people). This is the case for both positive and negative images.[36] The TPJ is active when you put yourself in the shoes of the other. You imagine how the other feels in that situation.[37] In most people, the TPJ is especially active when it concerns a stranger. When they put themselves in the shoes of a loved one, the ACC and insula are mainly activated.[38] In highly sensitive people, this distinction does not seem so strong. When they look at their happy partner, in addition to the ACC and insula, the TPJ is also strongly activated and vice versa, the insula is activated when they look at happy strangers.[39] Apparently, highly sensitive people consistently use the entire toolbox here too. In social situations, highly sensitive people empathize with others and use all 'social' areas of the brain. In this way they collect a lot of information regarding the social context. About their position in relation to the other, about possible 'social mistakes' and about the common experience. This could explain why highly sensitive people often indicate they can read social contexts easily.

I had the opportunity to lead project Z. It was something I really wanted. Due to my ability to put myself in other people's shoes and to consider the consequences for the social setting, I turned down the offer. I think it was the right decision for the department.

On the other hand, this major capacity to relate to others can also be a pitfall. I can empathize with others so well that I no longer even allow myself to voice my own wishes. What would have happened if I had said, 'I would like to lead the project, but I also see risks for the proceedings of some other projects if I were to accept this offer'? I never thought about that for a moment. To me, my answer seemed to be the only logical one. However, just because my brain automatically analyzes the social context does not mean I have to follow the option arising from this.

I have become much more aware of my thoughts. And of the fact that I am the only one who can defend my own interests. If your empathy stands in the way from what you really need, because you already consider what the other person's reaction will be, then your quality will lose its purpose. Therefore, the large capacity to empathize and focus on the social setting are talents of highly sensitive people, but can also become pitfalls.

7.3 CHOICE OF ACTION

This chapter is about the processing of information in the highly sensitive brain. I have called the last step in this process 'choice of action.' All considerations (the analysis of risks and opportunities and taking into account the social context) ultimately lead to a choice: the action (or no action) that is chosen. Of course, the strict distinction in these steps is arbitrary. One thing flows into the other. Unconscious processes also play a major role. The distinction I make in this (and the previous) chapter between the processing stages of the highly sensitive brain is intended to clarify the different processes, not to separate them from each other.

The action already starts during processing. For example, an affective empathic reaction unconsciously activates autonomous body processes. Seeing someone in danger also increases our own heart rate and can trigger a stress response, such as fleeing from that danger.

The topic I want to address in this section is whether highly sensitive people come up with more or different actions than non-highly sensitive people. Does the intense processing of information set highly sensitive people apart from others in this regard? If a non-highly sensitive colleague was asked to lead project Z, would they reach a similar conclusion? Of course, non-highly sensitive people also analyze the risks and opportunities and take the social context into account, but their brains do not automatically process all information that way. They do not always employ the entire toolbox. What effect does using the complete toolbox have on HSPs? Do HSPs see more alternatives or more creative options?

Thinking creatively

There is no direct evidence that highly sensitive people think more creatively than non-highly sensitive people, but there are several indications that this is the case. Dietrich and Haider conclude that very little is still known about how the brain works when thinking creatively.[40] Research in this field is conducted from different angles and with different research methods, so there is hardly any agreement about which areas of the brain play a role in creative thinking. Based on their review, Dietrich and Haider assume that two brain networks play a role: the default mode network and the central executive network.[41]

The default mode network (DMN) is – as I described in chapter 3 – an area in the brain which becomes active when there is no focused attention taking place. Daydreaming, worrying, fantasizing, and introspection activate this area. It includes the medial prefrontal cortex (mPFC), the medial temporal lobes (MTL), the temporo-parietal junction (TPJ), the angular gyrus (AG), and the cerebellum, among others.

The central executive network (CEN) is active when you need to focus your attention on a specific task and it supports the executive functions. It consists of the dorsolateral prefrontal cortex (DLPFC) and several areas in the posterior parietal cortex (PPC).

The DMN is more strongly activated in highly sensitive people than in non-highly sensitive people. This has emerged from research into the processing of emotional images or faces.[42] And research into the processing of non-emotional information, such as looking for differences and assessing the length of a line.[43] How this can be interpreted exactly, is still unclear. The DMN is not only involved in creative thinking, but also in the aforementioned process of mentalizing. Is the activation mainly a confirmation of the optimal-option-ambition, which implies that HSPs naturally take the social context into account? Or does this also support the hypothesis that highly sensitive people are good at generating creative ideas?
An indication of this could be the better performance with regard to categorization in the Wisconsin card sorting test (WCST, see the box in section 5.3). People with the s/s genotype of 5-HTTLPR (the variation that is more common in HSPs) required less clues for proper sorting of the cards. This indicates greater cognitive flexibility.

Research by Volf and colleagues (2009) shows that people with the s/s genotype come up with more creative solutions.[44] They asked 62 students to complete two assignments. In the first, figurative assignment, they had to construct images out of incomplete figures. The second assignment looked at verbal creativity: they had to make as many sentences as possible with three given nouns. The solutions were rated for uniqueness: the less often that solution was given by a large control group, the more points the participants received for it. Students with the s/s variant scored higher on both figurative and verbal creativity.

An interesting area of the brain in this context is the angular gyrus (AG).[45] It is involved in complex language functions, such as reading, calculating, writing, interpreting what is written, and understanding metaphors.[46] In certain situations, the AG appears to be more strongly activated in HSPs. However, two comments are in order here. First of all, this has only been demonstrated in situations where HSPs looked at their partner.[47] The question is whether this involves a lot of creative thinking. Secondly, Pick and Lavidor conclude that it is precisely underactivation of this area that leads to greater creativity.[48] Excessive activation of the AG would actually stimulate strict application of rules and would be especially important in automating knowledge. It is therefore unclear what meaning should be derived from this. When we let highly sensitive people speak for themselves, 70% say they have a talent for creative thinking.[49]

The dorsolateral prefrontal cortex (DLPFC), which is part of the central executive network (CEN), is more strongly activated in HSPs when they look at their partner.[50] In addition to directing executive functions, this area is also involved in acting fairly and in creative thinking. Perhaps this activation is an indication that highly sensitive people like to come up with and carry out fair actions for their loved ones. However, with today's knowledge, this is guesswork.

A possible link between high sensitivity and creative thinking is latent inhibition. This is the ability to exclude stimuli that seem irrelevant (see also section 5.1). It ensures that we are not constantly overwhelmed. At a networking event, for example, you only focus on sounds and other sensory information relevant to you at that moment. A low latent inhibition means that you cannot exclude irrelevant stimuli properly. Some mental disorders, such as schizophrenia, have been linked to low latent inhibition. However, research by Carson and colleagues shows that low latent inhibition can also be a quality. People with high intelligence and low latent inhibition perform better on creative tasks.[51]

The extra information they perceive because they are less able to close themselves off is used to reach creative solutions. However, this connection only applies to people of high intelligence.
The link between low latent inhibition and creative solutions may also be relevant for HSPs. Highly sensitive people also have trouble locking out stimuli and perceive many subtle details. This ability, as has been shown for low latent inhibition, may encourage creative problem solving.

7.4 SUMMARY

Suppose you are asked to lead a project. If you are highly sensitive, you process all information related to that situation in depth. Your brain is trying to find the optimal option. In doing so, it makes an analysis of risks and opportunities: what can happen, which consequences can arise, and what are the effects of those consequences? The highly sensitive brain is also alert to signals from the social context. How do others react to my behavior? Do they consider my actions to be good or bad? The brain identifies possible actions that take all those interests into account as much as possible.

The highly sensitive brain is able to relate to the other, be it a loved one, or a stranger, and reacts strongly to objects or situations with an emotional charge. In all these emotion-evoking situations, those areas of the brain that make you aware of your position in relation to the other, of possible 'social mistakes' and of the common experience of the other are activated in HSPs. As with problem solving, HSPs therefore seem to switch on many brain areas at the same time and process information in depth, even in social situations. While the average person chooses a single 'tool', a highly sensitive person uses the entire toolbox.

The optimal-option-ambition is the focus of the highly sensitive brain to find the best possible solution given the situation and the social context. This is not a selfish choice, it is about finding the best option for the group. The interests of the social group seem to take precedence in the considerations of the highly sensitive brain. This is in line with the experiences of highly sensitive people, who indicate that their own interests are subordinate to those of the group – causing the necessary frustrations.

It is often helpful to realize that your highly sensitive brain is strongly focused on those social considerations – and that you always have a choice in how you deal with the information resulting from this brain process.

I could have told my boss about the impact I anticipated, but I could also have told him that I would really like to lead project Z. As a natural response, I pushed my own wishes aside in favor of the interests of the department. I could also have stated my own interests, in addition to those of the department. Perhaps there would have been another solution.

CHAPTER 8

Reacting

Halfway through the meeting, tears suddenly ran down my cheeks. From pure stress. Next week, the room arrangements in our department would change. The day before, the colleague with whom I shared a room had indicated she would rather be in someone else's room. 'It's nothing personal', she had said. I had trouble sleeping last night. What did 'nothing personal' really mean? What was it about me that made her want to sit with someone else? I also preferred to go to a different room. I was glad it was mutual, but still it felt like I had failed. It made me very insecure about my new roommate. There were two candidates that I could be placed with. I clicked with both colleagues. Would that be mutual? Wouldn't they soon feel like they were stuck with me? Would they get fed up? Would a tension arise that would make working impossible? I had already noticed that morning that I was being desperately nice to both of them, afraid of doing something wrong, which would probably lead to disapproval anyway.

During the meeting we discussed the plans for the move. Which rooms came first, where you could work until then, and all the rules regarding room use were refreshed. 'Do not water the plants yourself, empty your desk every night and kettles are strictly prohibited.' This triggered my

tears. These rules were not new. I had known them for a long time, but realized I didn't really follow all three rules. In the middle of a project, the piles of papers would remain on my desk for weeks. I was afraid I would lose track if I moved them to the cupboard. I always made tea myself in my room, because the tea from the machine was impossible to drink. And good tea was, and is, indispensable for a productive day. And those plants... they were always given the leftover tea.
Suddenly, I was awash with the feeling I was failing. Here too, I fell short. I couldn't empty my desk each day. What is more, I was a burden to my colleagues. I held everyone back. All those emotions together ran down my cheeks in the form of big fat tears. I took the gamble not to wipe them off because I was afraid it would attract attention. But they had already caught the attention of some colleagues. I received astonished looks. How on earth could the listing of some rules lead to tears? I couldn't explain.

This chapter focuses on 'reacting'. Highly sensitive people perceive a lot (chapter 5), consider (chapter 6), and process the information intensely (chapter 7). Then they react to the stimuli. Highly sensitive people experience more intense emotions, more stress and more impact than non-highly sensitive people. Their reaction is sometimes inimitable and they have a well-developed self-reflection. This reaction is illustrated in figure 8.1 by means of an icon, the arrow at the bottom represents self-reflection.

8.1 MORE INTENSE EMOTIONS

Do highly sensitive people experience stronger emotions than non-highly sensitive people when in a similar situation? My emotional response during the meeting is not the norm, to say the least. In many workplaces, tears are seen as an inappropriate expression of emotion. Yet it happened to me regularly. In those days, accompanied with a lot of shame. But holding them back didn't work, because my emotions overflowed.

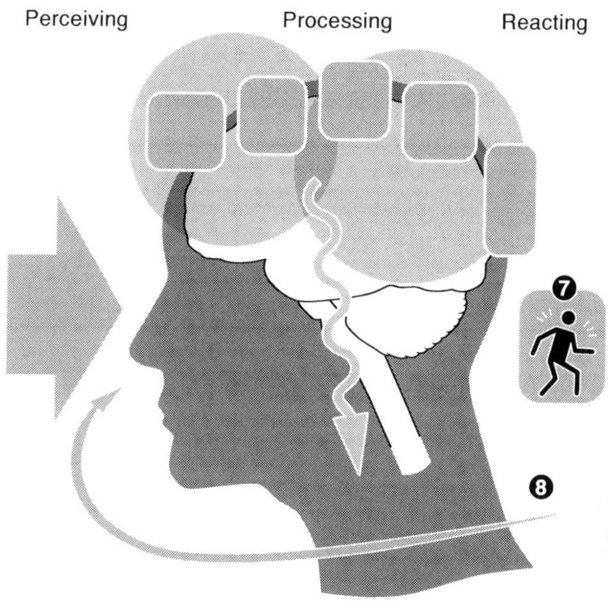

Figure 8.1 The highly sensitive brain: reacting

Jadzia Jagiellowicz examined whether highly sensitive people experience more intense emotions. In her 2016 article, she mapped the relationship between high sensitivity and emotional reactivity.[1] She asked 96 students to look at images on a computer. According to the HSP scale, 56 people in this group were highly sensitive and 40 were not. Each participant was shown 18 blocks of four pictures from the IAPS. Each block had a positive, neutral, or negative charge. After seeing the image, the students indicated which feeling it evoked in them to what extent, varying from 1 (= very negative), 5 (= neutral) to 9 (= very positive), and subsequently, how much tension the picture triggered on a scale from 1 to 9. In this study, a distinction is made between valence (feels something positive or negative) and arousal (how much tension it causes).

This study illustrates that all images evoke stronger emotions in highly sensitive people, when compared to non-highly sensitive people. This was the case with the negative and to an even larger extent with the positive images. A similar situation affects them more. However, despite the more intense emotions, the images did not evoke more tension in HSPs. Highly sensitive people thus respond to the same stimulus with more intense emotions.

In addition, the mood of highly sensitive people is more strongly influenced by stress. Elaine Aron and colleagues (2005) asked 160 psychology students to take tests in a classroom setting.[2] Several rows of separate tables had been formed. Without the participants knowing, the difficulty of one of the test pages differed.
The HSP scale, which they completed first, showed that 41 students were highly sensitive and 108 were not. In addition, their state of mind was addressed and questions were asked about other character traits. The first test pages inquired about their interest in art and knowledge of sports. Those pages were the same for everyone and were completed at the same time. The third page was the actual experiment. It contained questions related to intelligence. These questions were very easy for the participants in the even rows, but extremely difficult for the participants in the odd rows. This difference in difficulty was also evident from the scores. The easy version was completed in time by 84% of the participants, while only 34% succeeded with the difficult version. However, for Aron, it was not about performance, but about the effect on the mind. To what extent does it affect you if you see fellow students take a test with great ease while you are struggling? Does it affect your mood?
The following test page asked about the students' feelings in that moment. The data shows that the highly sensitive people felt much worse if they had taken the difficult test. Among the non-highly sensitive students, no difference was found between those who took the easy and those who took the difficult test (see Figure 8.2).

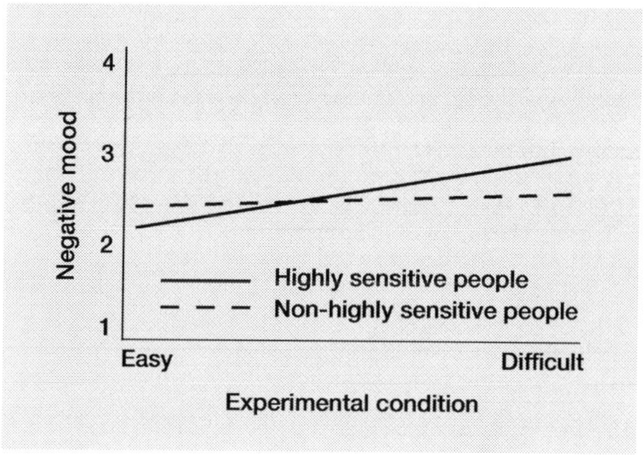

Figure 8.2 The influence of a negative experience (an experimentally evoked stressor) on the mood of highly sensitive and non-highly sensitive people (Aron, 2005)

The mood of highly sensitive people is thus influenced by an evoked stressor, while it had no impact on non-highly sensitive people. In addition, we have already seen that they experience emotions much more intensely. Although HSPs sometimes perceive their increased emotionality to be a disadvantage, emotions are an important aspect of decision-making.

Lerner and colleagues (2015) demonstrate that the idea that emotions primarily disrupt rational decision-making should be revised. For example, people who do not experience emotions due to brain damage make irresponsibly risky decisions. Emotions demonstrate what we deem important and color the situation. That information is used in our decision-making, both in the contents of our thoughts, in the depth of processing and in the link to our unconscious goals. In addition, it turns out that the more intense our emotions are, the more motivation we have to achieve those unconscious goals. Thus, emotions play a role in our judgment and decision-making.[3]

8.2 MORE STRESS

The in-depth processing of information seems to lead to more stress. Earlier I described that HSPs perform better on visual tasks. Gerstenberg (2012) asked subjects to search for a T in images filled with distractors. Highly sensitive respondents scored better on that task, but also experienced a greater increase in stress when taking that test.

Research by Thomas Boyce and his colleague Abbey also shows an increased stress response. Boyce describes their research in his book *The orchid and the dandelion,* in which he substantiates the environmental sensitivity of orchid children (also see the box in chapter 1).[4] Boyce and Abbey designed stress-inducing tasks for children between the ages of 3 and 8. These tasks should not be too overwhelming, but they should evoke a degree of stress: a conversation with an unknown adult, a drop of lemon juice on the tongue, or watching an emotional video. They measured the amount of stress through the amount of cortisol in the saliva and by monitoring heart activity.

The intensity of the stress response differed between the children. A small group barely had a stress response, a large group scored average and a small group had a very intense response. The highly sensitive children had a stronger stress response than the so-called dandelion children (the non-highly sensitive children).[5] Highly sensitive people thus experience a more intense stress response than non-highly sensitive people, when they are in the same situation.

This profound stress response does not stand alone, but appears to be the downside of the talent for being able to read social signals. This has been demonstrated by research into genetic variations in the oxytocin receptor. In short, oxytocin is a hormone that is involved in attachment.[6] The hormone is produced in the hypothalamus, the brain area that is also involved in the production of stress hormones (nor) adrenaline and cortisol. The effect of the hormone oxytocin depends on the oxytocin receptor (OXTR) a person has. OXTR comes in two different variants: A and G. Given the fact that everyone has two of these genes (one from the mother and one from the father), there are three genotypes: AA, AG and GG.

Rodrigues and colleagues researched people's empathic qualities and linked these to their genotype.[7] They found that people with the GG variant scored better on empathy tests and also state to have a high degree of empathy themselves. However, other studies show that people with the GG variant are more sensitive to social exclusion, are more likely to develop depression, are more affected if they have experienced early childhood neglect, and are more likely to have an insecure attachment style as adults. Ward concludes that people with the GG variant are better able to read social signals, but are also more susceptible to social stressors that are present for a long time.[8] This conclusion resembles the results of research on people with the s/s variant of 5-HTTLPR (the variant highly sensitive people are more likely to have). They too appear to be more prone to depression and other social stressors.[9]

The research by Sturge-Apple and colleagues (2012) provides a link by looking at both genes.[10] They examined the influence of conflicts between parents on their parenting style. They questioned parents about the conflicts they had with their partner and their parenting practices. Both the mothers with the GG variant of OXTR and the mothers with the s/s variant of 5-HTTLPR appear to be more affected by their environment. They become more sensitive to their child's needs and less punitive when there are fewer conflicts between the parents. And vice versa: in case of more conflict, these parents are more punitive and less sensitive to the needs of their child. The parenting style of other groups of parents is not affected by the presence or absence of conflict.

Thus, in terms of parenting style, the people with a GG variant of the OXTR gene are similar to the people with the s/s variant of the 5-HTTLPR gene. Both groups are sensitive to their environment. They can attune themselves well to the other, but are therefore also sensitive to stressors. In chapter 9 I will discuss the stress system further and in chapter 10 social stress and its effects on highly sensitive people are central.

8.3 MORE IMPACT

Highly sensitive people thus experience more stress because they are so influenced by their environment. But that effect is also present in the positive sense. When the conditions are right, they benefit more from a situation.

Michael Pluess used the term vantage sensitivity for this.[11] Vantage sensitivity means: taking great advantage of positive circumstances. For a long time, research has focused on the question of why some people suffer much more from adversity than others. Why are some people vulnerable and others resilient while going through the same unpleasant circumstances? Pluess focusses on the opposite: who benefits more from positive situations?

For example, it appears that some teenage girls with depressive symptoms do not really feel better after of an anti-depression intervention, while another group of girls clearly improves. The second group therefore has a higher vantage sensitivity: they benefit from the intervention. Moreover, this effect is permanent.[12]

The same result came from a study regarding anxiety disorders by Eley (2012). More than 350 children between 6 and 13 years of age with an anxiety disorder underwent cognitive behavioral therapy. All children benefited in this situation, but one group improved more than the rest. Often, their anxiety disorder even ceased to exist. The group with the highest advantage are those children with the s/s genotype of the 5-HTTLPR gene. 78% of these children no longer had any symptoms of anxiety after treatment. Among the children with the s/l or l/l variant this percentage was lower, namely 58%.[13] This difference is still visible during follow-up. Researcher Thalia Eley concludes that people with the s/s variant are able to derive long-term benefit from an intervention.[14]

The effect of positive situations on highly sensitive people is also visible when you consider their childhood. Already in the first study by Elaine and Art Aron into high sensitivity, there was a difference between highly sensitive people who had a good childhood and those who had a negative childhood.[15] Of the more than 300 respondents in that survey, one third of the HSPs indicated to have experienced an unpleasant childhood. These highly sensitive people with a bad childhood scored higher on social introversion (shyness) and emotionality (experiencing many negative emotions). The group that had a pleasant childhood (two-thirds of the HSPs) scored much lower on these characteristics, namely just as high as non-highly sensitive people.

Boyce also looked at this effect for children and their relationship with their teacher.[16] He established a link between health at age 13 and the support or conflicts they had with their teacher 6 years earlier. The dandelion children functioned on average and the relationship with their former teacher had little effect. Psychological and physical issues appeared to occur much more frequently among orchid children who had experienced many conflicts with their teacher at the time. The orchid children, however, who had maintained a pleasant, supportive

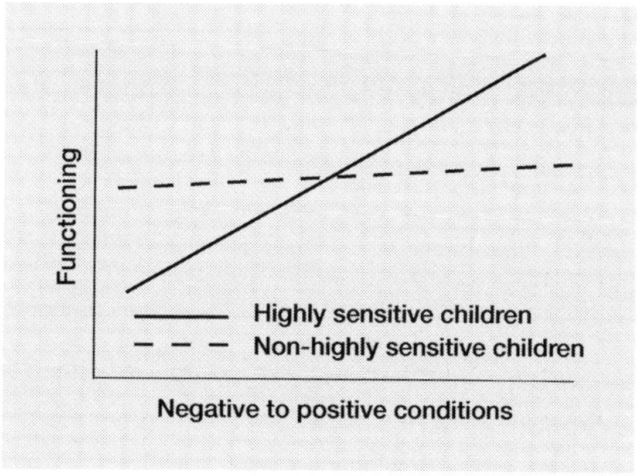

Figure 8.3 Highly sensitive children function worse in negative circumstances and better in positive circumstances

relationship with their teacher, had very few issues. Thus, the learning environment also has a two-sided effect on highly sensitive children. Bad circumstances cause more issues, while a good situation is more beneficial than for the average child.

In the highly sensitive brain, the differences between highly sensitive people with a good and a bad childhood are also visible. In 2017, Acevedo, Jagiellowicz, Marhenke, and the Arons conducted a study into the brain response of highly sensitive people to emotional photos, where they distinguished between childhood experiences (see box). This research shows that some brain areas are even more activated in highly sensitive people with a pleasant childhood.

Emotional stimuli and a good childhood

Bianca Acevedo, Jadzia Jagiellowicz, Robert Marhenke, Elaine Aron, and Art Aron studied the response of (non) highly sensitive people to emotion-evoking photos in 2017. This time, they also made a distinction according to childhood experiences. To gain insight into childhood experiences, the researchers used a weighted average of different questionnaires. Participants completed the Parental Bonding Inventory and the Measure of Parenting Style, both with regard to their father and mother, and a questionnaire (developed by Aron[17]) about how they experienced their childhood. The researchers calculated a single score using these results, which they call the Quality of Childhood Parenting (QCP). When they talk about 'people with a good childhood', this means these participants scored high on all these questionnaires. They are generally positive regarding the parenting style of and the relationship with their parents.

Fourteen students – exactly half of them highly sensitive – who differed in how they experienced their childhood, participated in this study. Their brains were scanned while they looked at emotion-evoking photos. They were shown six blocks with four positive, negative, or neutral photos each. After each block, they were asked how much tension they experienced on a scale from 1 to 7.
This provided a wealth of information about the functioning of the highly sensitive brain. One of the conclusions is that the brains of highly sensitive people with good childhood experiences react differently to both positive and negative images than that of HSPs with a bad childhood. Both groups also differ from non-highly sensitive people. The brain areas that are more strongly activated have to do with assessing social position, rewarding, the alignment between brain and body, and emotion regulation. In short, highly sensitive people with a good childhood seem to get more reward from social contacts, they are even more focused on the social context and better able to regulate their own emotions and physical reactions.

I subdivide the differences in the brain between highly sensitive people with a good and a bad childhood by type of image. The positive images activate other areas than the negative images.
In highly sensitive people with a pleasant childhood, many areas of the brain are activated more strongly by positive images.[18] Especially striking are the stronger activation of the insula, the areas with mirror neurons (inferior frontal gyrus and temporo-parietal junction), the medial prefrontal cortex, and the ventral tegmental area (VTA).
The insula is more strongly activated in all highly sensitive people when they process positive pictures.[19] However, the effect is greater in highly sensitive people who have experienced a good childhood.[20] In

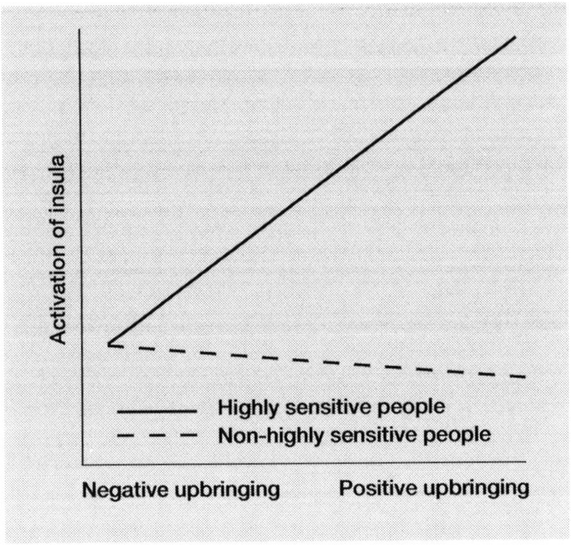

Figure 8.4 The activation of the insula in relation to upbringing and high sensitivity (Acevedo, 2017)

non-highly sensitive people, the childhood experiences have no effect on the degree of activation of the insula (see figure 8.4).

Since the insula is involved in many processes, this outcome can mean several things. Possibly, interoception works better for highly sensitive people with a good childhood. Due to their supportive upbringing, they may be better able to use their more sensitive interoception effectively. The stronger activation of the hypothalamus supports the reasoning that highly sensitive people with a good childhood are better able to regulate body signals.

In addition, it could also indicate a better empathic attunement in highly sensitive people with a good childhood. They may be able to use the ability to empathize with others (which all HSPs have) more when it comes to positive emotions. This is supported by a stronger activation of the mPFC, IFG, and TPJ. These empathic areas are more strongly activated in all highly sensitive people, but even more so in HSPs with a good childhood. For example, it appears that the IFG is more activated with positive facial expressions, but not in positive images in general, except for HSPs with a good childhood. They also have more strongly activated mirror neurons in generally positive images (of people, objects and situations) than non-highly sensitive people.[21] Possibly, when it comes to positive situations, HSPs with a good childhood can empathize even better than the average highly sensitive person, who in turn, can empathize better than the average non-highly sensitive person.

A new area that stands out when it comes to HSPs with a good childhood is the ventral tegmental area (VTA). The VTA is part of the brain's reward center and registers whether an event is rewarding or disappointing.[22] The VTA is strongly linked to the ventral striatum and orbitofrontal cortex. These determine, in various ways, the reward experienced with a certain stimulus.[23] The VTA is activated when you eat good food, when you receive a monetary reward, but also when you see your mother or partner.[24] Highly sensitive people who have experienced their upbringing as positive, appear to have more activation in this reward area when they look at positive images.[25] So they get more reward from these situations than the average person.

These results are in line with research by Moutsiana (2014). Christina Moutsiana and her colleagues followed children in a longitudinal study that lasted 22 years.[26] When the children were 18 months old, the child's attachment style was objectively determined by the researchers. They were re-examined at the age of 22. An fMRI scan was made of 54 participants while they looked at emotion-evoking images. The children with secure attachment had stronger connectivity between the prefrontal cortex and the reward areas, while this connection was lacking in children with insecure attachment. Apparently, a supportive childhood enhances the degree to which rewards are obtained from situations.

It is possible that a correlation exists between the stronger empathy and the greater reward in social contacts which we saw in highly sensitive people with a good childhood. They may enjoy pleasing their loved ones because the happy response they receive in return is a great reward for them.[27] This makes further developing their capacity to empathize even more worthwhile.

Also with images that evoke negative emotions, some areas of the brain are more strongly activated in highly sensitive people with a pleasant childhood.[28] What is striking here is the strong activation of the amygdala in relation to non-highly sensitive people. The amygdala is more strongly activated in all highly sensitive people when they look at fear-inducing images such as snakes or fire.[29] However, this is even more true for the HSPs with a happy childhood. Stronger activation of the amygdala is associated with more intense emotions. At the same time, the medial prefrontal cortex (mPFC) is also more strongly activated. It nuances – as I described in section 7.2 – emotions by reflecting on the experiences of others and thereby stimulates the realization that you are not the only one who is struggling.[30] The ability to empathize with negative situations also remains present in highly sensitive people with a good childhood. The average HSP has a reduced activation of the IFG (the area where mirror neurons are located) and an average activation of the TPJ (cognitive empathy) in negative images. Both areas are more strongly activated in HSPs with a good childhood than in non-highly sensitive people.

HSPs with a good childhood therefore experience even stronger emotions in negative situations and continue to empathize with others. After all, they get more rewards from these contacts and seem better able to regulate their emotions. This higher reward can be deduced from the activity present in the ventral tegmental area (VTA). Normally, negative emotions provide little reward in the brain. The study by Acevedo (2017) shows that the higher the score on the HSP scale is, the lower the activity in the VTA is with negative photos. However, this is different for highly sensitive people with positive childhood experiences. Pictures that evoke a negative emotion do not lead to a decrease in the activation of the reward areas in this group.[31] Highly sensitive people with a pleasant childhood therefore not only get more rewards from positive images, but also from negative images. They experience strong emotions, but know how to regulate those emotions well and can also remain attuned to the other.

In short, highly sensitive people experience more impact, both in negative and positive situations. HSPs with a good childhood seem to be even more focused on empathizing with others and receive more rewards from situations. But even if the start of life was not great, highly sensitive people are able to benefit from positive circumstances. The environment has a lot of impact on them.

8.4 INIMITABLE

The fact that others cannot always follow the reaction of the highly sensitive person is understandable now that you know how information is processed by them. Highly sensitive people process stimuli in depth, integrate information, empathize with the other, and connect information to previous events. The conclusion of all this processing might well be very different from that of someone who acts directly. The highly sensitive person has, so to say, taken a turn somewhere that was invisible to the other and ends up at a different location.

The reaction can be difficult to understand due to the intensity of emotions, but also because of the logic behind it. From the other's point of view, the final reaction may not be related to the initial situation. Testimonies of experiences illustrate how much this can lead to misunderstandings or irritation.

A link to creative thinking is also present here. One element of this concerns coming up with solutions others do not see. There are indications that highly sensitive people come up with more creative solutions (see section 7.3). This talent can sometimes go unnoticed, because the proposals are too inimitable to others.

8.5 SELF-REFLECTION

The ultimate act does not necessarily end the depth of processing. Even after the decision, action, or lack thereof, the highly sensitive person continues to consider the available information. The newly created situation provides fresh information, which is added to the analysis: the interpretation of the look on the other's face or of the reaction of those involved – it is all food for thought.

Their own actions in particular are subjected to a sharp investigation. Self-reflection is a beautiful quality, a requirement to be able to learn. Therefore, HSPs can potentially greatly improve themselves. The downside of this, however, is that they become too critical and disapproving of everything about themselves. Self-reflection can then evoke fear of failure and thus put a brake on further development.

8.6 SUMMARY

The fact that I had tears running down my cheeks was especially embarrassing to me. I was not aware of how my highly sensitive brain worked and mainly felt that I had to act 'normal'. The fact that I couldn't hold back my tears made me feel helpless and every time I felt them sting again, it added to the pressure: I-cannot-cry! Which of course was exactly what happened.

Highly sensitive people experience situations differently to other people. They pick up a lot more information and think about it more deeply. The emotions a situation evokes are therefore more intense. They feel more than others.

At the same time, highly sensitive people experience more stress. This is related to the depth of processing and to one's own (self-critical) thoughts. Unpleasant situations therefore have a major impact on a highly sensitive person. A stressful situation has a negative effect on well-being and welfare.

Fortunately, the opposite is also true. When the move was finally behind us and I had created a pleasant work room with a roommate, with whom I connected really well, I noticed that my functioning improved considerably. It seemed like everything became easier to me. All those negative and insecure thoughts were gone. I enjoyed the beautiful view, the pleasant atmosphere, my bigger cupboard (for all those piles of papers) and the fun projects I ran – and worked much more effectively than in the period before.

CHAPTER 9

Stress, the Brain, and Emotional Literacy

I finally had the courage to call in sick. After years of walking around with serious symptoms, I couldn't take it anymore. The pain in my hip made both walking and sitting unbearable. However, the expected peace of mind was still lacking. Now that I was home, I continued to worry about making the deadline for project A and the constant delay of the start of project B. I feared the disagreement between employees X and Y would erupt and wondered whether employee Q was being trained properly.

On top of that, I had new concerns. What if my hip issues were permanent? Suppose I would never be able to do sedentary work again. What could I still do? And what would it mean for my children if I were to remain limited in my mobility? Would I be able to take care of my children? How would that affect their development? What will the family dynamic be like due to my issues?

I saw hundreds of scenarios looming over me, the vast majority of which were negative. It made me want to fully commit myself to my own improvement. I worked overtime. Exercises for my hip, back, and arms. Maintaining a fixed daily routine. Keeping the house in order as well as possible. Considering how I would handle problems at work when I started again. And of course, as the company doctor had advised, I had to do fun things. Activities that were, of course, useful as well as fun. That seemed most efficient to me. I saw my illness as a project I had to bring to a successful conclusion.

I was at home to recover from my symptoms. I didn't have to get up early now, no long journeys to meetings around the country, and no more late night preparations. The workload was gone. In its place, the burden of my own thoughts increased. I unintentionally put pressure on myself. My mind and body remained alert and barely recovered.

I have endured the consequences of chronic stress and experienced how stress can be invisible. Highly sensitive people experience more stress as I wrote in chapter 8. In this chapter I demonstrate how the stress system works and how it relates to the highly sensitive brain.

9.1 STRESS

'Stress arises when the demands from your environment are greater than what you think you can handle,' said George Fink.[1] He composed a handbook on stress, wherein various definitions of stress are outlined. This definition immediately makes tangible what stress does to you. The biological definition of stress is much more technical (I explain the technical terms below): 'Stress is any stimulus that activates the HPA axis (which produces ACTH and cortisol) and the SAM system (with the accompanying release of adrenaline and norepinephrine).'[2]

In simpler terms, it says here: When you perceive something that seems to be beyond your ability to handle, your body sends a signal to the hypothalamus. This brain area activates both the HPA axis and the SAM system.

HPA-axis

The HPA axis is the abbreviation of the technical term hypothalamus – pituitary – adrenal axis. For the sake of convenience, I use the term HPA axis.

When a stressor is detected, the hypothalamus signals the pituitary gland using the neurohormone CRH, which then produces adrenocorticotropic hormones (ACTH). Through the bloodstream this travels to the adrenal gland, which produces cortisol.

Cortisol is called a stress hormone, but it mostly plays a facilitating role. It ensures that energy is released in the body so the stress hormones adrenaline and noradrenaline can do their work. Cortisol releases that energy, among other things, by breaking down proteins in muscles and by putting the immune system and digestion on the back burner. All that released energy is needed to respond to the perceived threat. Cortisol also ensures that your body settles back down. Namely, it inhibits the production of ACTH and CRH, enabling the axis to regain equilibrium.

SAM-system

The hypothalamus also stimulates the production of adrenaline via the so-called SAM system. This abbreviation stands for sympathetic-adrenal medullary system. It is a fast connection between the hypothalamus, adrenal medulla, and the autonomic nervous system. The autonomic nervous system controls the self-regulating functions of organs and glands. The adjacent somatic nervous system controls the voluntary movements of skeletal muscles. The autonomic nervous system consists of an accelerating (the sympathetic nervous system) and a decelerating part (the parasympathetic nervous system). The hypothalamus sends a signal to the sympathetic part of the autonomic nervous system, which stimulates the adrenal medulla through the nerve pathways to release adrenaline and noradrenaline. That nerve connection is much faster than the HPA axis bloodstream. This is useful, because adrenaline and noradrenaline help you respond to perceived threats. They prepare your body for action by speeding up breathing and heart rate, increasing blood pressure, enlarging pupils, and making you perspire.

Acute or chronic stress

The HPA axis and the SAM system ensure that you can respond to the stressors you perceive. That you can fight against injustice, flee in case of a fire, or freeze behind a cupboard during a shooting: the so-called fight/flight/freeze response. The stress system is therefore essential for our survival.

However, problems arise when stress hormones are continuously present. In that case, the physical systems no longer settle down and energy is continuously extracted from muscles, the immune system and digestion. This makes you more likely to get infections and the flu, or suffer from muscle pain or stomach issues.

The hormone cortisol, which takes care of these processes, also has an effect on the brain. Long-term high levels of cortisol result in more activity in the amygdala, less activity in the medial prefrontal cortex, and less volume of the hippocampus.[3] It therefore affects the regulation of our emotions, our memory and our ability to put things into perspective.

The hippocampus and cortisol mutually influence each other. The hippocampus is a kind of limiting device for cortisol production. Similar to speed limiter in a car, the hippocampus sends a signal when a certain amount of cortisol is reached. It signals the hypothalamus to stop production. If cortisol is present for too long, the hippocampus' feedback mechanism stops working and does not inhibit the production of cortisol. Moreover, this hormone reduces the volume of the hippocampus, causing the limiter to function even less well.

This effect has often been examined in research on depression. A study by Schmaal and colleagues (2016) shows that people with depression often have a smaller hippocampus.[4] This subsequently causes problems in the executive functions and, in particular, in cognitive flexibility: you are less able to adjust when an error occurs.[5] Reduced hippocampal volume is also associated with learning and memory problems. You no longer remember your pin codes or you forget appointments. Professor Hickie, one of Schmaal's colleagues, explains in an interview that your self-image is also affected. Due to a smaller hippocampus you put less of yourself and the world around you into perspective. You therefore perceive yourself differently.[6]

A smaller hippocampus also affects how you respond. The hippocampus stores the contextual information of a memory, framing the event. In case of chronic stress, the hippocampus shrinks and the amygdala, which provides memories with emotional color, is more strongly activated. As a result, you experience events more intensely: the emotional color dominates the context. It is difficult to put events into perspective and you become emotional quickly. Causing you to be more inclined to experience situations as stressful, allowing chronic stress to persist. Acute stress is useful because it helps us get ourselves to safety, while chronic stress sustains itself and depletes our system (both physically and mentally).

Obsolete stress system

In their book *Van big bang tot burn-out* (From big bang to burnout), Witte Hoogendijk and Wilma de Rek state that our stress response system is failing us. Our stress response is still the same as when we were fish. If you need to flee from a shark, it works really well. But we experience similar stress responses in case of unexpected noises, payment reminders, or notifications on social media. In fact, we do not merely become stressed due to concrete stressors, but with abstract ones as well. This concerns thoughts such as: What if I cannot get another job? What if

my partner leaves me? Or: What would the neighbor think of me? The brain does not distinguish between concrete and abstract stressors. Whether a lion comes your way or you think your partner does not like you anymore, the stress system switches on the whole nine yards. Your body is being prepared for action. When the lion has disappeared, the system settles down again. But when do your concerns about your relationship disappear? Those thoughts remain and ensure a continuous activation of the stress system. Essentially, it uses a sledgehammer to crack nuts.
Hoogendijk and De Rek describe how this excessive stress response causes numerous psychological, psychiatric and somatic illnesses: depression, burnout, PTSD, anxiety disorder, addiction, high blood pressure, heart disease, et cetera. In addition, somatic conditions such as psoriasis and herpes simplex are triggered by stress.

So our stress system doesn't seem quite suited to the challenges of our society, with its continuous flow of information, noises, and expectations coming our way. The highly sensitive brain, as I showed in the previous chapters, registers more stimuli and uses more energy to process these. In addition, it is attentive to the expectations of others and to the prevention of errors. In other words, it signals many concrete stressors and also creates a flow of abstract stressors. As a result, the stress system of highly sensitive people is likely to be switched on more often. Lisa Feldman Barrett's work can shed even more light on the connection between high sensitivity and stress.

9.2 PREDICTIVE BRAIN

In her book *How emotions are made,* Lisa Feldman Barrett shows that stress and disorders such as chronic pain, anxiety and depression are closely related due to the functioning of our brain.[7] She has summarized this in the so-called prediction loop (see box).

Prediction loop

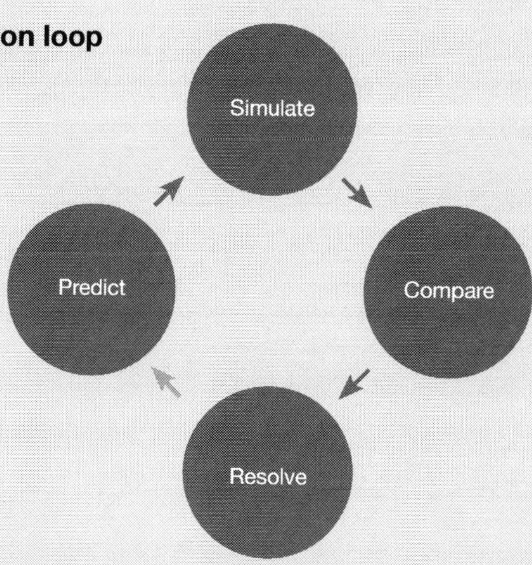

Figure 9.1 The prediction loop by Lisa Feldman Barrett (2017)

When you walk in the forest and you see a bush moving, in a split second, your brain makes a prediction based on prior experiences. For example, that a wild boar will approach (predict). This prediction prepares the body for action (simulation). The activated stress systems cause you to feel your heart beat faster, your hands become sweaty, and you start breathing faster. Your brain then compares the more detailed sensory input to its preliminary conclusion. Is there indeed a boar approaching? Or was it a stray dog, or maybe just the wind? (compare). Our brain is not very good at that. Sometimes we see the boar, when in reality, no boar is present.
If, in that forest, we notice that a wild boar is actually running towards us, our body is already prepared to run away. In case there is no wild boar behind the bush, the brain makes new, better predictions (resolves). The stress system settles down again. In approximately 30 minutes, the stress hormones will have left your body.

Misinterpretation by the brain

The body needs resources such as oxygen, glucose, salt, and water to function. It transports these resources to the necessary places. For example, when your body digests food, your digestive system uses resources from your muscles. And if you have to use muscle power, the energy for that is extracted from other body parts. Your brain predicts which resources your body needs and controls the transfers. When your brain makes wrong predictions, it creates an imbalance.

Feldman Barrett explains that if the imbalance continues to exist, your brain misinterprets this as a demand for energy. It then continues to release energy, which can cause your body systems to hit the red. If this continues for a long time, we call it chronic stress. Feldman Barrett refers to it as chronic misbudgeting. As a result, the distribution of the body's resources does not match with what is really needed and a recovery delay arises. Furthermore, the brain changes due to chronic misbudgeting.

Cortisol plays a major role in this process. As I wrote in the previous section, this stress hormone releases energy to respond to the perceived threat. If your brain mispredicts the need for energy too often, you will have too much cortisol in your blood. This has an effect on your hippocampus, but also on so-called cytokines.

Stress and immune system

The messengers between the brain and the immune system are called cytokines. These are proteins that release signals via the nervous system regarding enhancing or moderating inflammation. The pro-inflammatory cytokines create swelling and high temperatures to signal the body that energy is needed for recovery. They make you feel tired and feverish and make you want to withdraw.[8] So they're very useful if you have been injured.

Normally, cortisol suppresses the development of inflammation. But if cortisol is present for a long time, that ability decreases. Chronic stress means long-term high levels of cortisol, which means that cytokines cause more inflammation and fatigue, when there is no actual need for this.

That's when the problems really start, says Lisa Feldman Barrett. Because you feel tired, you exercise less. Your brain thinks it saves energy with this, but has misinterpreted that there are too few energy supplies. You also eat more to supplement your (non-existent) deficiencies, causing your balance to tip even further. Moreover, this imbalance creates sensations with a very unpleasant affect; you feel miserable. The cycle also strengthens itself when you gain weight due to the combination of eating more and exercising less. Certain fat cells produce pro-inflammatory cytokines, which increase inflammation.[9] Because the cytokines stimulate you to withdraw, you hardly see other people and you feel more and more alone and excluded. Additionally, inflammation can also develop in the brain. This affects your ability to remember things and focus your attention. Neurons may even wither and die. Most importantly, inflammation in the brain due to cytokines affects your prediction cycle.

The third step in the prediction cycle is to compare the prediction to the actual sensory input. Feldman Barrett indicates that the brain does not always listen to that sensory input. That is why we sometimes think we see something which is not there at all, like that wild boar in the bushes. It is also the reason why many witness statements are not very reliable. Of all the court rulings in the US that were later proven to be false on the basis of DNA testing, 70% were based on witness statements.[10] Judges rely on eyewitnesses, while our brains are quite prone to mistakes.
Inflammation caused by cytokines increases this; these make the brain virtually deaf to corrections. Your brain therefore continues to base itself on prior predictions and unnecessarily transports bodily resources. For example, in the case of the wild boar, your brain does not listen to the sensory input that it was just the wind that made the bushes

move. The brain thinks optimal readiness is required, speeds up your breathing even more, tightens your muscles, and makes your heart pump even faster. This action mode is unnecessary because there is no threat. However, the energy for this preparation has already been used and your body needs recovery time. With abstract stressors (our thoughts about difficult situations) the same effect occurs. Even then, your body needs time to recover. If you do not take that recovery time, you will have less and less energy.

If your brain continuously predicts stressful situations without being corrected by safe reality, the cortisol level remains high, the cytokines cause a lot of inflammation and you constantly feel tired and unpleasant. This system – of chronic imbalance and rampant inflammation – is the cause of many disorders, according to Lisa Feldman Barrett: depression, anxiety, obesity, insomnia, heart disease, diabetes. According to her, the distinction we make between these conditions is arbitrary. All these conditions involve mismanaged resources due to chronic imbalance. Your brain is driving you to do the wrong things, which makes the problems worse. The link that Hoogendijk and De Rek make between stress and common illnesses is thus specified by Feldman Barrett. She shows that a malfunctioning prediction cycle, with incorrectly controlled body resources and inflammation as a result, is the basis for the development of these disorders.

9.3 THE HIGHLY SENSITIVE BRAIN PREDICTS, PERCEIVES, AND REVISES

How does the prediction cycle function in the highly sensitive brain? This has not been studied directly, but I suspect that the highly sensitive brain makes many more predictions than the average brain. This hypothesis seems to be supported by the increased activity of the default mode network (DMN) in highly sensitive people.[11] This network is active when no conscious task is being performed, for example while daydreaming. It is also the place where predictions are generated.[12] Since the brain predicts on the basis of previous observations and highly sensitive people perceive a great deal and link those observations to prior knowledge, it is likely that their brain makes more (detailed) predictions.

More predictions

That can be an advantage and a disadvantage. Too few predictions means the body is not put on alert. Feldman Barrett suggests that autism spectrum disorder (ASD) could be a condition in which the brain makes too few predictions and therefore becomes overwhelmed by sensory input.[13] Research by Acevedo, Aron, Pospos and Jessen (2018) illustrates that the highly sensitive brain is clearly different in this regard. They analyzed the differences in brain activations and discovered that (among other things) the default mode network was more strongly activated in highly sensitive people and less so in people with autism.[14]

However, many incorrect predictions are also problematic. Those incorrect predictions unnecessarily or incorrectly relocate resources within the body. This can lead to chronic misbudgeting, resulting in illness. If the predictions are accurate, the body is consistently in an optimal condition for the situation in question. Predictions are more likely to be correct if you have more concepts and more emotion words at your disposal (see section 9.4).

Simulation

The next step in the prediction cycle is simulation. Based on predictions, the body simulates the accompanying sensations. If you think you see a wild boar, your heart rate and breathing speed up. Through simulation, what your brain thinks it perceives matches what you experience in your body. I do not expect any differences between highly sensitive and non-highly sensitive people in this regard. At the most,

I can imagine that simulations occur more often in highly sensitive people, because more and/or more detailed predictions are made. After all, the simulation is driven by your predictions: the better the prediction, the better the simulation.

Compare

The sensory input is only absorbed consciously after the body has been prepared for action. The brain then compares that information with the prediction it has made. If the input matches the prediction, the deployed processes will continue as usual. In chapter 5 I described that highly sensitive people are more observant: they register subtle information others do not see. They also seem to rely less on routine. In fact, research by Aron (2010) showed that for HSPs, the cultural differences between Americans and Asians do not play a role in problem solving. They did not experience more difficulty with problems that did not match the way of thinking within their culture; they solved all issues in the same profound way. Thus, when it comes to perception, highly sensitive people seem to be less guided by existing concepts. As a result, their observations are possibly more neutral. This implies that HSPs perceive sensory input faster and more neutrally. They are likely to ignore sensory input less often and be open to information beyond their fixed concepts.

The perceived information is compared with the prediction. Is there really a wild boar? Or is it the wind? If the prediction is in line with the sensory information, the deployed processes continue. If not, the next step takes effect.

Resolving

If the sensory information differs from the prediction, the brain adapts. It uses the sensory information to make a new prediction that is better suited to the situation, so the body prepares properly. For example, if you get on your bike to go to work, just like every other morning. You have already made this journey hundreds of times and know how to avoid every loose tile and take all the turns blindly. In the first corner, however, you suddenly feel yourself slipping. You had not noticed the ice. Your brain receives new sensory information and adjusts the body accordingly. You feel your heart beating faster, you suddenly see the ice on the pavement very clearly and feel your muscles tighten. Like a true equilibrist, you make it through the bend in one piece.

It is pure guesswork regarding how this works in the highly sensitive brain. In general, I expect that the combination of many predictions and a lot of sensory input will lead to frequent adjustments. The interpretation of the observation and the correctness of the predictions determine how this plays out (see also section 9.4 on emotional literacy). If the predictions are not specific enough for the actual situation because the perceived sensory information is not properly interpreted, the adjustments are also inaccurate. Although the system is constantly resolving, the wrong processes are triggered. A chronic imbalance then arises, accompanied by fatigue, unpleasant feelings, and physical issues. A feeling of unrest may also be experienced due to the constant adjusting.

A great deal of resolving has a different effect if the prediction cycle works accurately. The highly sensitive person perceives sensory input in detail, adjusts errors and makes an appropriate prediction. In this situation, the brain also adapts. Only this time the body is transporting energy sources to the right place. This results in a healthy balance and pleasant feelings of energy and control.

Worrying

Our own thoughts – the demands we set for ourselves or worries we have – can also be stressors. If we have reoccurring worries, our brain perceives these as useful concepts for predicting situations. Worrying thus increases the chance of faulty predictions. These predictions are often not corrected by sensory input. As these thoughts often consider 'what if' situations and this hypothetical situation is often distant. This worry therefore continues to transfer body sources and puts the body in a state of alert unnecessarily. Chronic imbalance develops. In burnout literature, worrying is therefore seen as the first sign of an approaching burnout.[15] In such a case, learning to break through the worry cycle and learning to recognize the signals from inside and outside the body in the moment is a first step towards a healthier balance.

9.4 EMOTIONAL LITERACY

The highly sensitive brain probably produces many and detailed predictions. It then simulates the corresponding physical reactions. All subtle details the highly sensitive brain perceives in the environment are used to adapt and adjust the predictions. However, this self-correcting cycle can lead to chronic stress and illness if the brain makes wrong predictions. It improperly prepares the body.

Predictions are more likely to be correct when you have more concepts and emotion words at your disposal. Feldman Barrett (2017) calls this emotional granularity, or emotional literacy. Being emotionally literate means being able to use precise emotion words at the right time. You interpret the situation appropriately, so that your brain receives the correct instruction. If you are only able to give a broad meaning to what you feel – such as feeling good or not – then the instructions given to the brain are not specific enough. Your brain may immediately switch on the stress system if you 'don't feel well'. People who can identify nuances within an unpleasant feeling give more precise instructions to the brain. After all, fear is different from nervous or vigilant. The facts show that being able to pinpoint your emotions exactly has a major effect on your health. It has been shown that people with high emotional literacy see a doctor less often, take less medication, and are admitted to hospitals less frequently. They also drink less alcohol to relieve stress and react less aggressively to people who have hurt them. People with low emotional literacy are more likely to report depression, eating disorders, borderline, and autism.[16]

Being emotionally literate – being able to categorize intricately – means knowing many emotion words and being able to state them whenever applicable. The technique even works as anxiety therapy. Kircanski, Lieberman and Craske (2012) let people with a fear of spiders undergo various therapies. The subjects were shown a real spider and had to apply one of the four techniques.

1. While observing the spider, some of them had to describe what emotions the animal evoked in them (affect labeling, i.e. describing in words what they feel).
2. Another group had to relabel their feelings (give a different value to their emotions, for example, relabel 'afraid' to 'challenged').
3. The third group had to distract themselves (distracting oneself from the bad emotions).
4. The final group was simply put in contact with the spider and did not use any technique.

Of the four groups, the people who applied affect labeling had fewer stress responses (measured by conduction in the skin). All these people had done was describe the feelings they experienced by seeing the spider. Describing your emotions in a fearful situation thus lowers your stress over time. This effect turned out to be greater if the words used were better suited to the situation. People who had used fear and tension words more often in the exercise had fewer fear responses when the subjects encountered the spider again a week later.[17] Thus, having many emotion words at your disposal works better to alleviate a fear of spiders than commonly used techniques such as cognitive relabeling and distraction.

Even with drawing, this effect is visible. Thomas Boyce (2019) researched the immune system of children on their first day of school

after the summer vacation. For some children, this transition resulted in a deterioration of their immune systems. A month after school started, there was an earthquake in the area, which of course was an even greater stressor for the children. The researchers made an inventory of how many children became ill in the following weeks. The children who experienced a major change in their immune system after the start of school were more likely to suffer from colds and ear infections or pneumonia in case of a major stressor. They identified this group as the highly sensitive children.
They then asked the children to draw a picture of the earthquake. The orchid children, as Boyce calls the highly sensitive children, more often made gloomy drawings. Instead of happy figures in vivid colors, they drew fearful faces and damage to their homes and used dark colors. In the weeks after the earthquake, it turned out that the children who had made the fearful drawings had far fewer respiratory diseases. This was contrary to expectations, because the highly sensitive children had a stronger response in their immune system. However, the connection with the drawings was stronger. Boyce concludes that children who experience emotions intensely benefit greatly from expressing their emotions in any form.[18] It is helpful and healing for them to share their emotional experiences.

I am convinced that highly sensitive people will be especially able to apply many nuances when identifying their feelings. They feel more intensely. An important condition is that they have learned useful concepts, for example from their parents. And that is certainly not the case with everyone. If you do not have those concepts at your disposal, you quickly interpret a sensation as your own shortcoming. For example, many women interpret menstrual issues as being emotional issues, while these are in fact periodically recurring physical signals.[19] Or imagine that you just had a fight with your partner. Suddenly you experience chest pain. Is it a heart attack, heartburn, fear of abandonment, or anger because your partner was unreasonable? In this case, the right concept helps you to take the right action: call the ambulance, take an antacid, talk it over with your partner, or stand up for yourself.

Emotional literacy may also explain the differences between highly sensitive people with good and bad childhood experiences. Highly sensitive people who experienced a lot of support in their childhood possibly felt free to express their emotions as a child and thus developed a wide vocabulary. As a result, their brain may be better able to make good predictions and their body is properly prepared for action. The stronger brain activations of highly sensitive people with a pleasant childhood are perhaps explained by this (see section 8.3). They may be better able to interpret the sensations they experience. In socially uncomfortable situations, for example, they understand what is going on and that it has nothing to do with them. As a result, they are able to benefit from social contact and regulate their body in the right way.

Emotional literacy can be taught. If you have not been properly equipped from an early age, you can enhance it yourself. On the one hand, you have to perceive your body signals well and, on the other hand, have enough concepts to interpret these. You can train yourself to be aware of your body signals with different approaches, such as yoga, mindfulness, or psychomotor therapy. You can expand your emotional dictionary by describing more precisely what you experience, or by reading a lot about how others experience something. Reading novels, watching movies, sharing experiences with others, writing, drawing, making music, these are all ways to learn how to express emotions more precisely. This way, you help your brain to formulate the correct instructions, your body is better balanced and you feel more energetic and healthier.

9.5 SUMMARY

I started this chapter with this definition of stress: 'Stress arises when the demands from your environment are greater than what you think you can handle.' I then discussed how stress arises and addressed the role of the brain and the physical consequences of chronic stress.

Highly sensitive people experience more stress. This seems logical when you look at the highly sensitive brain. The first element of the definition covers 'demands from your environment'. If you notice more (because you notice subtle details), more 'demands' will come your way. On top of that, there are the social demands and your own demands. Highly sensitive people perceive social demands strongly, because they are so focused on the interests of the social group. The expectations of others are therefore important to them. Their own demands arise from a strong self-reflection: there is always room for improvement. This means the perceived demands can be higher than what a non-highly sensitive person would experience in the same situation.

The second element of the definition is 'what you think you can handle.' This has to do with how you look at a situation, how you interpret it, and what the brain predicts to be necessary. I have shown that many more predictions are likely to take place in the highly sensitive brain than in the non-highly sensitive brain. If those predictions and any adjustments are correct, then a highly sensitive person will be able to deal well with the demands he experiences. If not, however, an imbalance in the system occurs and chronic stress develops. The highly sensitive brain continues to adjust based on incorrect predictions and detailed input, which increases feelings of fatigue and illness.
The key here is emotional literacy. The highly sensitive brain can benefit greatly from this. By giving words to the sensations you experience, you are giving your brain commands. The more accurate they are, the better the brain can prepare for the situation. Stress situations can be better interpreted, allowing the body to initiate the correct processes. A finely tuned machine is then created which can handle everyday challenges.

CHAPTER 10

Social Rejection and Self-compassion

'What a disaster,' I said to my friend. 'I relived the party all night long. I'm not leaving the house anytime soon. I am so embarrassed.'

That weekend we had attended a neighbor's birthday party. A large group of women, about half of whom I knew, shared hilarious stories about their children that night. My friend was having a lot of fun and I had a difficult time getting her to leave.

For me, the evening had felt endless. I do have a sense of humor, but telling funny stories is definitely not my specialty. I was put on the spot by a mother from school when she said, 'Esther, tell the story of that weird incident you had at school with your kids lately.' Well, it's not like everything was smooth sailing for me, but I really couldn't remember any weird incidents. I stammered a bit until she concluded that 'I apparently felt too good to share the story.'

The evening went on. Everyone had fun. But those words kept going around in my head. *Did she think I felt too superior to share the story? I simply didn't know what incident she was referring to. If she thinks I feel 'too good', she may think I'm arrogant. Maybe the others think so too. I have to prove that's not the case.*

I tried to reconnect with the group, but noticed that no one responded to my comments, that no one even brought a drink along with them for me. Or was I just imagining this? Did I create a bigger problem in my head? I became very aware of everything I was doing. Tried to drink as normally as possible, enjoy some cheese, laugh along. But nothing felt normal. My cheeks ached from the artificial smile I had on my face. I perceived everything as a rejection by the group. I was not one of them. I was excluded.
At home in bed, in my memory I saw even more rejections in the body language and looks from others. I felt myself getting smaller and smaller. Suddenly it occurred to me what incident she was referring to. My embarrassment grew even more from the idea that those women now thought I had deliberately not wanted to share that particular story. It would only confirm their view of my so-called arrogance. They would exclude me even more. I resolved never to return to the schoolyard.

The highly sensitive brain is more sensitive to stress. Social stressors are a great source of stress. For everyone – we need the group to survive – but especially for highly sensitive people. After all, they are much more focused on the social context and social stress has a strong effect on them. Social rejection is the most painful form of this. Stress can easily put a highly sensitive person into a self-reinforcing cycle of social rejection. In this chapter, I will exemplify this process. Shame, a counterproductive emotion that can maintain the self-reinforcing cycle, will also be addressed. The chapter closes with the 'antidote': empathy and self-compassion.

10.1 SOCIAL STRESS

Belonging to a group is important for every person. We are social animals. We need social contact to survive. If this is compromised, it can trigger a stress response. Fight and flight stress responses are the most familiar. When you experience a threatening situation, the stress system releases energy to be able to: fight to defend against the threat, or flight to avoid the threat. The third stress response is freezing. With this response, there apparently is no option to fight or flee, and you curl up on yourself (literally or figuratively) to limit the damage caused by the stressor.

Psychologist Shelley Taylor studied laboratory animals under stress and discovered that mainly the males fight or flee, but the females use a different strategy.[1] They are often focused on protecting and nurturing their offspring, among other things, by entering into social networks. She called this stress reaction tend and befriend. This response has also been demonstrated in humans, in both women and men (the latter to a lesser extent).[2] In threatening situations, they seek protection and comfort from the group. That is one way to increase your chances of survival.[3]

When you are strongly focused on friendships and taking care of others, this may concern a stress response. If you experience social stress during a party, as I do in my example, as a response you may get drinks for everyone, attentively inquire about the worries of others, calm arguments, etc. In this way, stress leads to social behavior.[4]

Cortisol plays a major role in the fight and flight stress responses. The hormone oxytocin is important in the so-called tending and befriending stress response. The production of this hormone is, among other things, triggered by the hypothalamus. When more oxytocin is present, less fear is experienced, repose ensues, and the tendency to nurture is enhanced. Oxytocin calms the HPA axis and thus reduces the stress response. However, the opposite effect has also been shown. Oxytocin increases the attention to social signals and can therefore also cause more stress and/or aggression.[5] After all, sometimes a protective strategy can be perceived as aggressive by outsiders. Additionally, people who are perceived as threatening are sometimes excluded from intimate relationships. Thus, the tending and befriending stress response can provide positive effects (more nurturing and calmness) or negative effects (more alertness to social signals, aggression and/or stress) to both oneself and their environment.

Thomas Boyce demonstrated the effect of social stress on highly sensitive children. One of the biggest social stressors in a young child's life is the first day of kindergarten. The child has to deal with social insecurities (how is my behavior received by the group), expectations (of himself and the teacher), and of course an abundance of germs. He therefore utilized this moment in various studies. He linked that moment to the social stress the child experienced at home.
During the summer holidays, two weeks before the first day of school, Boyce and colleagues drew blood from 5-year-olds. After the first day of school they repeated this. This allowed them to measure the effect of this first day on their stress level. In this study too, they found that orchid children had the greatest stress response; their cortisol levels had increased. However, that did not necessarily mean that these children also developed more illnesses. Only the children who also experienced social stress at home (measured by means of a survey among the parents) and were highly sensitive, developed more respiratory diseases. Here too, they saw that highly sensitive children who experienced little social stress at home were the healthiest.[6] The degree of social stress therefore has a major effect on highly sensitive children. In this case a physical effect, but Boyce has shown that the memory is also affected.
In another study, Boyce demonstrated the link between social stress and memory. Children from 4 to 6 years of age took part in this test. The researchers who conducted the interviews were divided into two groups. Some researchers were (consciously) very nice and empathetic. They made the children feel comfortable and created a pleasant environment. Other researchers were (consciously) very surly. They talked distantly and matter-of-factly. They had a short chat with the children while making hot chocolate for them. With marshmallows. And rainbow sprinkles!

However, while boiling the water the fire alarm went off. After the sound of the alarm, the children were reassured directly, all in the same way. There was no fire. It was probably the steam coming from the kettle. The researcher would then continue preparing the chocolate milk, following a fixed set of actions.
A division was made between orchid and dandelion children, based on their cortisol reactivity.
Two weeks later the children were invited again. A new researcher asked them about the events from last time. They were given open questions, such as: 'tell me everything about what happened last time', or direct questions, such as: 'how many marshmallows did you have in your chocolate milk?' The dandelion children knew very well what had happened. Their memory did not appear to be influenced by which researcher they had met, the nice one or the surly one.
For the orchid children this was different. They appeared to be heavily influenced by the social stress the distant researcher had evoked in them. The highly sensitive children who had encountered a surly researcher, could hardly recall the events from two weeks before.[7] The highly sensitive children who encountered a kind researcher appeared to have an exceptional memory of what had happened, remembered the exact order of events and the exact formulations. They even knew things the researchers no longer remembered, such as the clothing worn by the researcher.
These studies demonstrate how much effect social stress has on highly sensitive children, in terms of health and memory.

A test designed to measure social stress in adults is the so-called Trier Social Stress Test (TSST). This measures the stress response of people when they are judged by stand-offish members of a jury while barely being prepared (see box).

Trier Social Stress Test

This test was designed in 1993 by Clemens Kirschbaum and colleagues of Trier University, in order to measure the physiological effects of stress evoking tasks. They chose tasks they could standardize, so other researchers could easily copy the experiment. The main elements are speaking in front of an audience, conducting a mathematical task, and anticipating an evaluation. Before the test starts, devices are attached to the participant in order to measure his blood values and heart rate. Next, he is taken to a room where a panel of three judges is waiting with a video camera. The judges have a neutral look on their face and act stand-offish. The participant is requested to give a five-minute presentation in five minutes. The topic of the presentation is often the adequacy of the participant for a certain job.

During the five-minute preparation time, the participant may use pen and paper to prepare his presentation. This paper is unexpectedly taken from him the moment he has to present in front of the jury. During the five-minute presentation, the judges do not comment, they maintain their neutral expression. They do request the participants to complete the five minutes, if necessary.

Directly after the presentation the participant must conduct a mathematical sequence. They must count back from 1022 in intervals of 13. If they make a mistake, they must start over. This section also lasts five minutes.

When the test is over, the participants are informed of the test objective. They are told that the results of the tasks do not say anything about their competences.

The stress responses varied between people. Approximately 30% did not have an observable stress response. In the other 70% a (large) increase of, among other things, cortisol and ACTH was measured.[8]

For a lot of people, the stress evoking tasks of the TSST are probably enough reason to cause stress: doing a presentation after just five minutes of preparation time and reciting a complicated mathematical sequence. Research by Dickerson and colleagues (2009) indicates that performing these tasks in front of a jury makes it especially stressful.[9] They modified the TSST a bit and asked two groups of participants to prepare a speech. One half spoke in front of a panel of experts, as in the usual format. The other half delivered their speech alone in a room. The people who had to speak before a panel had a greater increase in stress. This was not only apparent from the increased cortisol levels, but also from an increased pro-inflammatory activity. This activity by cytokines, as I wrote in Chapter 9, occurs in stressful situations. It is the body's way of signaling that it needs recovery. This study demonstrated that the more people felt judged, the stronger the cytokine activity is. So if you feel you are being judged or rejected, inflammatory activity increases.

While some people experience only a very small stress response from this social stress test, there is also a group that is so strongly affected that inflammatory activity increases. There is even a group that gets a stress response just by observing other participants.

The research by Buchanan and Preston (2016) clarifies the effect of a large capacity to empathize on the transfer of stress. In that study, a second group of participants was added. The first group took the test as usual. Each participant from the second group observed someone from the first group. The stress level of those observers was also measured. The first striking result was that observed stress could also lead to stress in the observer. The cortisol level does not increase just like that, so the observers must have experienced stress themselves. The second remarkable finding concerned a link between the increase and the level of empathy of the observer. Those who scored high on empathy (this was measured by questionnaires about empathic involvement and the ability to empathize with someone else) were found to have a stronger

stress response. Moreover, this stress response was linked to the stress of the participant they observed.
The more stress someone else experiences, the more people with a great sense of empathy also experience that stress themselves. From this we could conclude that highly sensitive people, who are after all very sensitive to the emotional state of others, are influenced by others' stress. Another important conclusion is that the more you feel judged or rejected, the more inflammatory activity occurs in your body.

10.2 SOCIAL REJECTION

To better map the link between social stress, cytokines and the feeling of rejection, Slavich combined two tests. He let participants perform both the TSST mentioned in section 10.1 and the cyberball game (see box in section 7.2). Slavich and colleagues asked 31 participants to give a spontaneous speech to a panel of dismissive, unresponsive reviewers and subsequently scanned their brains while playing the cyberball game.[10] The participants with a stronger increase in inflammatory activity during the speech also appeared to have more brain activity in the ACC and the insula during the cyberball game.[11] These brain areas are involved in social rejection and the experience of pain. Being rejected is therefore just as painful as physical pain.
Therefore, in this study by Slavich, a link has been shown between the presence of cytokines and activation of brain areas that detect social rejection.

Naomi Eisenberger and colleagues (2017) summarize the relationship between cytokines and social behavior in their article 'In sickness and in health: the co-regulation of inflammation and social behavior'. For many years, it was assumed that the immune system has little to do with controlling social behavior. In the past few decades however, it has become clear that these strongly influence each other. Inflammation appears to increase the neural sensitivity to negative experiences. Rejection and negative social feedback are then perceived more strongly. One possible explanation for this is that, from an evolutionary point of view, it is important to remain part of the group, especially when you are sick.

On the other hand, as Eisenberger demonstrates, infections also strengthen reward areas in positive social experiences. People with a lot of cytokine induced infections are more likely to approach their loved ones and family. Makes sense when you consider they are the ones who will have to take care of you when you are sick.

Inagaki's (2015) research simulated that situation.[12] He administered endotoxin to subjects, resulting in a pro-inflammatory response. At the height of that inflammation, these people (compared to those who received a placebo) reported much more often that they wanted to be with their loved ones. When Inagaki showed them pictures of their loved one, the first group showed greater neural activation of the ventral striatum. This brain region – as I described in Chapter 3 – responds to rewards. The stronger the inflammatory response, the stronger the activation of this reward area when the subjects saw a photo of their loved one. Thus, when you are sick, it is more rewarding to be with your loved one.

Eisenberger and colleagues (2017) illustrate that social stress and pro-inflammatory activity stimulate each other.[13] When someone has more negative social experiences or feels left out, the level of measured inflammation increases. Social stress therefore magnifies the inflammatory activity. The inflammatory activity then causes the brain to detect threats to social connection earlier, which further increases social stress (see box).

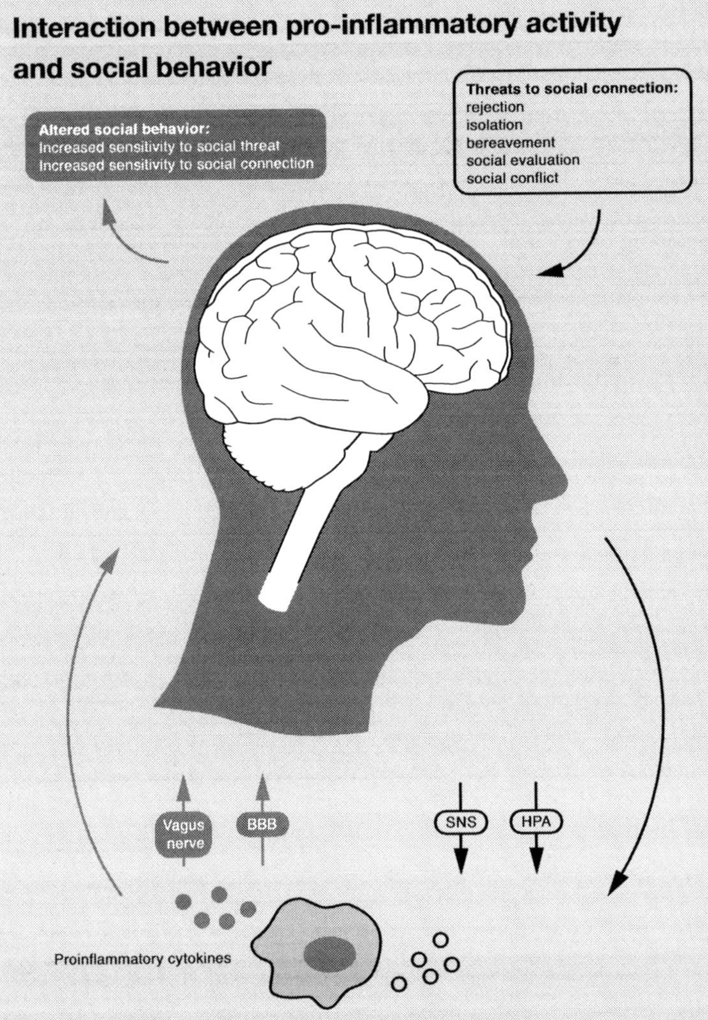

Figure 10.1 How pro-inflammatory activities and social behavior influence each other (Eisenberger, 2017)

Naomi Eisenberger shows that pro-inflammatory activity and social behavior influence each other. The left side of figure 10-1 shows that pro-inflammatory cytokines through, among other

things, the neural pathway (vagus nerve) and the blood-brain barrier (BBB) signal the brain to change the neural sensitivity to the social environment. This leads to an increased sensitivity to social threat and social connection. The right side shows that situations that threaten social connection (rejection, exclusion) activate the sympathetic nervous system (SNS) and the stress axis (HPA axis), increasing pro-inflammatory activity.
This creates a self-perpetuating cycle. More chronic stress leads to more inflammation, which leads to more attention to social threats, making these more likely to be noticed, causing the person to experience more exclusion, which causes more stress, leading to more inflammation, et cetera.[14]

Rejection sensitivity

According to Eisenberger, sensitivity to rejection arises from pro-inflammatory activity caused by chronic stress. She approaches this topic from a biological perspective.

Geraldine Downey studied the same subject with Scott Feldman, but from a psychological perspective. They wondered what effect cognitive-affective processes have on the success of romantic relationships. They studied how lovers interpret each other's behavior and what effect it has on the relationship. People who interpret unwanted behavior from their partner as conscious rejection show an overreaction that affects the relationship. Downey and Feldman call this rejection sensitivity. People with high rejection sensitivity fear that others may not meet their need for acceptance and connection. However, their response to what they see as evidence of that fear causes them to behave in a way that makes the relationship worse.[15]
Downey and Feldman argue that this behavior originates in childhood. They base this on Bowlby's attachment theory. He assumes that children

develop a mental model of themselves and their relationships based on their experiences. That mental model varies according to the degree to which caregivers have consideration for or reject the child's needs. When caregivers reject the child's needs, the child develops a model in which he is insecure and doubts whether others will accept and support him. Compared to people who assume others will accept them, people who expect rejection behave more hostile and aggressive in relationships. When they are actually rejected, they experience more loneliness, social anxiety, and depression.[16]

There does not seem to be any difference in secure attachment between highly sensitive and non-highly sensitive people. On average, about 58% of people are securely attached, according to a review by Bakermans-Kranenburg and Van IJzendoorn in which more than 10,000 adults were examined.[17] Research by Aron shows that two thirds of the highly sensitive people indicate they had a pleasant childhood.[18] This is not exactly the same as being securely attached, but it does make it plausible that the figures for HSPs are unlikely to deviate.

The effect of the home situation does appear to be greater on highly sensitive people.[19] For a highly sensitive child who is naturally alert to the social setting, an unsafe home situation means many perceived stressors and ultimately chronic stress. He becomes extremely alert to rejection and experiences a lot of stress. Dealing with this has priority over learning and developing.

Highly sensitive children who have a supportive home situation experience support when they need it and learn that their needs matter and are fulfilled. These children are just as focused on the social setting, because their highly sensitive brain excels at this. However, they get different information from the context: they experience support and acceptance. A review by Groh and others shows that children with secure attachment are more socially competent.[20] As a result, they may be better able to put into words what they experience. With what we know about the predictive highly sensitive brain, this means that completely different body processes are set in motion. The stress system is not activated, but body resources are used to deliver performance. This highly sensitive child has plenty of room to grow.

In summary, what can we conclude about the relationship between high sensitivity, stress and social rejection? Highly sensitive people have a stronger stress response in the same (social) situation. In itself that is not a bad thing. Stress is also useful, because it helps us deal with the situation. Several studies also showed that highly sensitive children can thrive despite prior stressful experiences, namely when the circumstances are supportive. They often perform even better. If those conditions are not right, or if the brain's predictions are not correct, then the stress will lead to issues. When that stress subsequently becomes chronic, it leads to an increase in inflammatory activity. This has the additional effect of a greater sensitivity to rejection.

Highly sensitive people are already more sensitive to social context and social rejection than non-highly sensitive people. This has a strong effect on them. In a situation of social stress (in a non-supportive environment), it appears that they develop more issues and perform less well on memory tasks. In these situations, it is likely that highly sensitive people more often enter the self-reinforcing cycle of social rejection.

If you suffer a lot from rejection sensitivity, you are always anxiously awaiting rejection, you are strongly focused on signals of rejection and you react disproportionately when you are actually rejected. Whether you look for the cause of this in attachment problems, such as Downey and Feldman, or in cytokine activity, such as Eisenberger, or in a combination of the two, it is a cycle that is difficult to get out of.[21]

Breaking the cycle

Our social environment triggers us continuously. This happens through actual interactions such as a reproach from a friend, but also through situations that you imagine yourself – *What if I am reprimanded by my boss?* – or through commercials – *Will others find me more interesting if I have this nice X*? These situations come to us in large quantities via social media. Via Facebook, Instagram, but also via direct messages. A message that has been sent, received, read, but not answered by the other releases a stream of negative thoughts. Vice versa, a received message gives us the feeling that an immediate response is required.

The highly sensitive brain is more focused on the social context than the non-highly sensitive brain. This can lead to a strong rejection sensitivity, for example because the person is not securely attached, but also to chronic stress. In both situations, you are even more alert to rejection and perceived rejection strongly affects you.

One way to break that cycle is to label your sensations differently. John-Henderson's research shows that your interpretation affects your body and your performance. If you are afraid of public speaking, your nervous system produces strange butterflies in your stomach, which you interpret as stress, resulting in the production of cortisol and cytokines. But if you interpret that same butterfly sensation as excitement, fewer cytokines are released. You feel less miserable and perform better.[22]
Using the right concepts for the situation thus improves your performance, as shown by this research as well. This also applies to all kinds of social situations. For example, what is your conclusion if someone has not yet responded to your message, even though it was read an hour ago? If you think you have done something wrong, your body interprets this as a stress signal and produces stress hormones. As I wrote in section 9.1, your brain doesn't differentiate between 'A lion!' And 'Apparently I did something wrong' – the whole stress system kicks in. However, if you conclude, 'This has nothing to do with me, maybe the person didn't have time or needs to think about it,' then the body does not produce stress hormones. Your interpretation therefore influences the effect a situation has on you.

Another way to break the cycle is to actually connect with others. Instead of believing what you think you see, namely rejection by the other, you can consciously choose to connect with the other. However, this is easier said than done. According to Brené Brown (2018), shame stands in the way of this process.

10.3 SHAME

There was a time where singer/songwriter Alanis Morissette felt ashamed of her high sensitivity. In the documentary Sensitive, the untold story, about high sensitivity, she shares her experiences with Elaine Aron. She often felt that people found her difficult. Too intense and too complex. But at the same time she was adored for the songs she wrote. 'They wanted the outcome of my trait, but not my trait.'
She tried to suppress or hide those highly sensitive sides of herself. Adapt to what people wanted. But she discovered that she needed her high sensitivity to write beautiful songs. She wrote the song 'That I Would Be Good' about wanting others to like her for who she is. 'That I would be good even when I am overwhelmed' is a line from this song. Alanis now knows that the artist does not exist without the highly sensitive Alanis.

An emotion that often accompanies the feeling of rejection is shame. My international research on HSPs at work shows that 35% often feel left out at work and 49% are ashamed of themselves. Whether these percentages are different in non-highly sensitive people remains unknown.[23]

Shame-researcher Brené Brown has written several bestsellers on the topic.[24] Her TED talk 'The power of vulnerability' has been viewed more than 35 million times. In her latest book, *Dare to lead* (2018), she writes that shame is the intensely painful feeling that we are not good enough and not worth loving or belonging. She calls shame counterproductive because it prompts us to withdraw from social contact and hide our real problems. We think that if we share these problems, others will find that we are indeed not good enough. We keep our vulnerabilities to ourselves to prevent us from being left out. We arm ourselves against pain, disappointment and rejection. But because of that armament we cannot establish a real connection.

In her book, Brown describes sixteen ways we try to protect ourselves, of which I share a few here.

1. Perfection and fear of failure. Perfection, she believes, increases the feeling of shame because it is based on the addictive notion that if everything is perfect, you can avoid painful feelings. Perfection sounds like a plus when it comes to performance, but according to Brown, it is mainly aimed at performing well in the eyes of the other. Healthy striving is the healthy form.
2. Assume scarcity and waste beautiful moments. When something beautiful happens, you may tend to expect something negative will occur as well. A promotion, pregnancy or engagement also evokes vulnerability, because it can come to an end. That is why we try to protect ourselves by not fully enjoying these beautiful moments and preparing ourselves for the terrible that will 'certainly' follow.
3. Sedation. We protect ourselves by numbing our feelings with alcohol, food, sex, games or television, among other things. However, we cannot selectively sedate. All emotions, the good and the bad, are muffled by it.
4. Postpone. Not doing difficult things so you cannot fail and will not be disappointed. Postponing will actually get you into more trouble.
5. Compensate for the pain you experience in a different way. For example, spending a lot of time at work where you feel useful because your partner pays too little attention to you. However, all that hard work will not bring you closer to your partner.

As humans, we thus develop armor that protects us from pain, but at the same time, form a barrier to connect. Shame keeps us from talking about our real desires. A culture of shame – within a family, organization or country – is a culture that promotes sickness, according to Brown. Remaining silent allows shame to proliferate. This leaves us with our bad feelings and we retreat further into our armor.

In Brown's view, empathy is the way to break a culture of shame. Empathy diminishes shame. The competences she deems important for being empathetic are taking the other's perspective without judging it, understanding the other's emotions, and communicating that understanding. The final skill that matters in empathy, according to Brown, is mindfulness. She refers to the art of letting emotions exist without exaggerating them. She borrowed this concept from Kristin Neff's theories about self-compassion.
Empathy is a talent highly sensitive people naturally have. The areas of the brain involved in empathy are more strongly activated in HSPs. As a result, they are well able to understand and empathize with others. Highly sensitive people can therefore play an important role in breaking through a culture of shame.

When it comes to breaking through their own shame, it is important that highly sensitive people also experience empathy from others. And that is a delicate point. If they are sensitive to rejection, the other person's behavior will be more easily interpreted as dismissive, and therefore less empathetic. Having a great sense of empathy even forms a disadvantage: you can well imagine what negative things the other person is thinking. For example, how the other judges you or how he is bothered by you. Having a lot of empathy can therefore dissuade you from talking about your own vulnerabilities.
We have little influence on the other person's empathic qualities. But as a child, we benefit from an environment in which these qualities are stimulated. Research by Thomas Boyce shows that highly sensitive

children perform considerably worse in classes with a strong hierarchy and where exclusion occurs, especially if they are at the bottom of the social hierarchy of the class. When this is the case, they report more psychological issues such as depression. However, if the teacher offers a counterbalance to the dynamic, the outcome is different. For example, when a teacher does not automatically choose the side of the most dominant child, if she acts against exclusion and compliments the talents of the children who tend to be left out. Highly sensitive children thrive in such a climate.[25]

We only have a limited influence on the empathic response of others. However, we do influence our own empathetic response. We call this self-compassion.

10.4 SELF-COMPASSION

The person who needs to approach you with empathy the most, hardly ever does. That person is you. Imagine: What do you say to a friend when he is fired, rejected or has forgotten something? Is your response disapproving or understanding? And what do you say to yourself in those situations? Are you compassionate or very critical of yourself? What words do you use when addressing yourself? And what effect do these words have on you?

While it may feel like you are boosting yourself up to do better when you are being self-critical, it actually has the opposite effect. Self-criticism has been associated with various psychopathological conditions and unhealthy relationships.[26] People who are self-critical feel inferior, not good enough and ashamed. As a result, they continuously experience the fear of falling outside the group and no longer belonging.

Kirstin Neff defines self-compassion as treating yourself with care and attention when faced with personal failures, mistakes, imperfections, and painful life situations. Self-compassion, according to Neff, consists of three scales:

1. Self-kindness versus self-criticism. Being kind, caring, and understanding towards yourself rather than being judgmental and self-critical.
2. Recognition of humanity versus isolation. Recognizing that being human means being imperfect. Everyone makes mistakes or fails and we all have our share of suffering to cope with. This realization prevents you from feeling isolated when you face adversity.
3. Mindfulness versus over-identification. Awareness of what is happening without judgment. Do not ignore your sensations, but do not overreact either.

Self-compassion can help reduce self-criticism, Neff writes. For example, a kind, compassionate response to a deficiency can lessen your sense of self-judgment. Recognizing that everyone makes mistakes helps reduce the feeling that you are the only one and therefore not good enough. Dealing with emotional pain mindfully helps you look for what you need, instead of blaming yourself for the situation.[27]

Compassion for the other comes naturally for a highly sensitive person, but what about self-compassion? A highly sensitive person has a high degree of self-reflection, therefore self-criticism arises quickly. You see everything you are not doing well. Self-criticism has an effect on your health. Facing your mistakes with compassion is an important step in keeping your brain and body healthy. Talk to yourself the way you talk to a loved one. Consider being your own loving parent, who is understanding, sees mistakes as part of life, and who does not run away from negative emotions. Identifying with that role is something highly sensitive people can do well and that is often an effective way to develop more self-compassion.

How important it is not to run away from your negative emotions, is also addressed by Elke Geraerts in her book *Het nieuwe mentaal* (The new mind) (2016), the follow-up to her bestseller from 2015 *Mentaal Kapitaal* (Better minds). Geraerts describes that many people feel like a failure when they experience negative feelings. This makes them question the choices they have made – and we make endless choices every day. This doubt results in a choice overload. Thus, they are left with the feeling that they are failing.

This is a feeling we like to suppress. Geraerts says: 'By repressing negative emotions instead of processing them, we make it impossible for ourselves to feel positive emotions and we allow the negative emotions to be expressed in the most inopportune ways.' The solution Geraerts provides for this is an approach that consists of emotional granularity, breaking through shame, paying attention to the positive and self-compassion.

Geraerts explains the term emotional granularity by using a metaphor of a photograph: a photograph in a higher resolution provides a sharper image. The higher your emotional granularity – or literacy – is, the more clearly you can distinguish between emotions. Brené Brown also emphasizes the importance of this. In her view, emotional literacy is crucial in building empathetic relationships.[28] A wide range of emotion words help you to understand the other better and enable you to communicate your understanding accurately with the other.

Emotional literacy therefore helps break the self-reinforcing cycle of social rejection in two ways. In section 9.4 I described the effect of emotional literacy on your health. By being able to give precise words to the sensations you experience, you are giving your brain accurate instructions for preparing the body. This prevents the so-called chronic misbudgeting and the associated increase in inflammatory activities in the brain which enhances sensitivity to rejection. The second way is through empathy and self-compassion. High emotional literacy makes it easier to understand the other (and yourself) and respond with compassion, keeping you connected with each other. This reduces your sensitivity to rejection.

10.5 SUMMARY

At my neighbor's party, I felt left out. I thought the others were judging me and saw small signals which confirmed that feeling. Everything else faded into the background. I was only concerned with the social group and how to get back into it.

Social stressors have a major effect on highly sensitive people. Their stress response is stronger than that of non-highly sensitive people. That fact in itself has little effect on their functioning. If the social environment is supportive, they can cope with stressful events. They even seem to flourish. But when the social situation is negative, this affects highly sensitive people to a large extent. These effects are reinforced by the fact that social stress increases inflammation caused by cytokines, while the inflammation in turn increases the sensitivity to social threats. One maintains the other.

This is extra difficult for highly sensitive people. They find real connection very important and their brain is especially suited for this. They have a high capacity to empathize and are strongly focused on social cohesion. At the same time, these talents increase their sensitivity to social rejection and their great ability to empathize can prevent them from sharing their own vulnerabilities.

Increasing self-compassion can be a way out of that self-reinforcing cycle. Self-compassion means treating yourself with care and attention when you are faced with personal failures, mistakes, imperfections, and painful life situations. It improves your health. Emotional literacy is also important here, being able to find precise words for what you feel. This makes it easier to share those emotions with others. And most importantly, it makes for better predictions by the brain. The brain then gives the correct instructions to the body, so the cycle of chronic stress and an increased sensitivity to rejection can be broken.

CHAPTER 11

Recognizing and Acknowledging Talents

I always felt 'different'. Now that I look back on a number of events in my life, I think that feeling was partially caused by the reactions I received from others to my behavior. The company doctor, who informed me that I was making it very difficult for myself to get better if I kept having these complicated thoughts. My colleagues, who advised me to take a week off because I cried during the meeting about the move. My friend, who told me not to take it so personally what had been said at my neighbor's party. My then partner, who did not understand why I came home feeling so exhausted from the work dinner at that Italian restaurant and that I had no energy left to go out with him.

From such responses I have always concluded that my behavior was strange, incomprehensible, or even problematic. However, I did not know any other way. I had no idea how to stop my complex thinking or how not to be bothered by something. Now that I understand more about the highly sensitive brain, I understand that too. My brain processes information much more deeply than others do. It involves information from many different angles and focuses more than average on the social context. As a result, I experience situations much more intensely and I need more recovery time.

Now that I know that non-highly sensitive people think in a different way, I also understand the reactions to my behavior better. Based on their own vision, my company doctor, colleagues, friend, and ex-partner gave good advice. The fact that I couldn't do anything with it was neither my fault nor theirs. We each had a different point of reference. It makes sense that one or both parties feel misunderstood. However, I think the effects are even more far-reaching. It also means that we do not always recognize talents. In this chapter, I will explain this and discuss the individual and social consequences thereof.

11.1 FORGOTTEN TALENT

Witte Hoogendijk, author of the book *Van big bang tot burn-out* (From big bang to burnout), expects the number of burnout cases to rise further in the coming years, because the number of stimuli in our society continuously increases. Digitization and social media are constantly expanding. According to Hoogendijk, there is a group in society that cannot cope with this. Without mentioning high sensitivity, he indicates there are 'cautious' people. He explains that each animal group has introduced specializations. There are animals occupied with hunting and gathering, but there is also a more cautious group that pays attention to the small signals, such as whether the berries are poisonous. This is in line with what Max Wolf concluded: within each species there is a group that is active and often impulsive and one that is more cautious and responsive. Both types are necessary for the survival of the species.[1]

The problem, according to Hoogendijk, is that we no longer see the benefits of that cautious group, namely the highly sensitive people. Behavior is judged by other standards. People who are cautious, Hoogendijk continues, are often told that this is a problem and that they have to take a pill for it. A pill for anxiety, insecurity, depression, compulsion, et cetera. This, however, denies the value of the behavior, according to the professor.

In my opinion, the talents of highly sensitive people are indeed not acknowledged enough. I think this is why a lot of highly sensitive people experience difficulties. It all starts with the environment recognizing their talents. Luk DeWulf, author of *Ik kies voor mijn talent* (Go with your talent), states that talent cannot be developed until someone has noticed it.[2] Therefore, he considers the acknowledgement of children's talents to be essential for their development.

If no one has ever mentioned the talents of a highly sensitive child, that child mainly mirrors himself with the talents of others. However, because his highly sensitive brain functions differently, these skills cost him a lot of energy. The child feels inadequate. The abilities this child naturally possesses are not noticed or perhaps even criticized. A child who treads carefully is categorized as shy and in need of assertiveness training. A child who is anxious in new situations has an anxiety disorder and will probably benefit from soothing medication. A child who is unable to concentrate because of all the stimuli he perceives must take Ritalin. And a child who provides unique answers needs to stay focused and do as asked. Instead of seeing the talent behind the behavior, the behavior is seen as problematic. Moreover, the proposed solutions often do not offer any long-term relief.

When the talent of a highly sensitive child is seen, this can make a world of difference. When a child is praised for his ability to observe a situation and recognize threats. When the child knows that his keen perception sometimes needs to relax for a while, so that it can then be used optimally again. And, especially, when the highly sensitive child is complimented for the ingenious solutions he comes up with. Then, even as an adult, he has access to this indispensable ability in our increasingly complex society.

11.2 INDIVIDUAL BALANCE

When highly sensitive people are confronted with a situation where they do not feel understood and feel unappreciated, it has a major effect on them. It affects their functioning. Four response patterns are possible at an individual level.

First of all, the highly sensitive person might conclude that he is apparently not talented and/or not worthwhile. That visual becomes his self-image. This can be seen as a freeze reaction: a stress reaction where the person freezes himself in the situation. He identifies himself with the image that is reflected from his environment. This often leads to a feeling of powerlessness. That feeling then increases social stress and thus maintains the vicious circle.

The second possibility is a flight response. The highly sensitive person tries to escape from the situation, for example by suppressing his negative feelings through addiction. As a result, he no longer feels how painful the lack of acknowledgement and understanding is, but he also cannot work on a real solution for those unpleasant feelings.

The third option is the fight response. By rebelling against people who do not see and understand his talents, he fights the unpleasant situation. He can get carried away. Overstate his talents. As a result, others tend to ignore him. This strategy is probably less common in highly sensitive people.

The fourth stress response is the tend and befriend strategy. The highly sensitive person can, for example, take good care of others, please them, and then hope to be seen as well. In her book *PRI en de kunst van bewust leven* (PRI and the art of conscious living) (2011), Ingeborg Bosch refers to one of the survival mechanisms she describes as 'false hope'. A nice summary of what this response is about. By tending/learning/performing well, you hope the other will give you what you need. The other person, however, often has no idea what your needs are. As a result, the balance of giving and receiving between you and the other feels even more skewed and the feeling that nobody understands and acknowledges you becomes even stronger.

All of these responses make a lot of sense when you consider how stressful the lack of acknowledgement and understanding is for the highly sensitive brain, which is focused on connection and social context. However, each response pattern aggravates the situation of misunderstanding. To break through this, an action is needed that does not arise from (social) stress. In my experience, four steps are essential in this regard: gaining insight into one's own sensitivity and the associated talents, learning to practice self-compassion and increasing emotional literacy, living life based on values that are important to you (instead of others) again, and finally learning new behavior.[3]

11.3 SOCIETAL BALANCE

The leader who has to explore an archipelago and has different animals in his team can complete his mission better and faster if he makes use of the talents of all his team members. Nonetheless, it often plays out like I described at the beginning of this book: those who cannot climb (or whatever talent is seen as ideal) are at best used for a supportive activity (gathering food) and at worst ignored (they just have to keep themselves busy). The fact that the fish can swim around the islands and therefore assess the situation is often not considered. In most cases, not even by the fish himself, because it is not always aware of its talents.

In any case, an important opportunity is being missed. As mentioned, animal research by Max Wolf shows that a responsive group consisting of about 20% of the population is essential for the survival of the species. And I think this is also true for humans: we need the different talents to stay balanced as a species, to ensure long-term survival. We have no use for people who can pick a lot of berries if we do not know which ones are poisonous and which are not. Nor do we have any use for people who can hunt wolves if we do not know how to catch them.

We need all talents. This sounds like a sine qua non. Everyone will agree. Yet, in practice, we often react differently. For example, in her book *Quiet,* Susan Cain illustrates that people often respond to job applicants from a certain ideal image. This means that people who are not outgoing have less chance of getting the job. We also assess the issues others experience from our own experience and knowledge. The issues experienced by highly sensitive people are therefore sometimes referred to as symptoms of diagnoses instead of as (sometimes temporary) effects of high sensitivity.

A first step to change is gaining more insight into the talents of highly sensitive people and how these can be used. After this, it is up to each family, team, group, and relationship to reach agreements; practical implementations where all parties do their best to understand the other and each individual feels appreciated for what he contributes.

11.4 TALENTS

Better insight into the functioning of the highly sensitive brain makes the talents of highly sensitive people more visible. Of course, everyone is different and each combination of traits brings a unique pattern of qualities. I address talents that, through the functioning of the highly sensitive brain, are naturally present in many highly sensitive people. Sometimes they are already well developed, sometimes they are potentially present but still undeveloped.

Figure 11.1 visualizes the highly sensitive brain. Based on the characteristics of the highly sensitive brain, I distinguish (at least) ten talents.

An important characteristic of the highly sensitive brain is the ability to perceive subtle stimuli related to physical stimuli, emotions and details (number 1). These three talents relate to this.

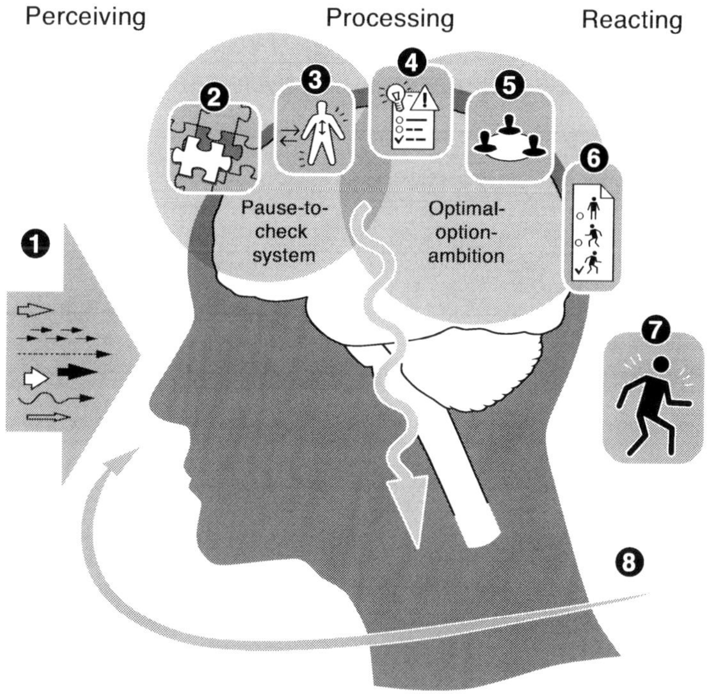

Figure 11.1 Visualizing the highly sensitive brain

1. Talent to perceive subtly

In a society where conclusions are drawn quickly, where presuppositions are made and witness statements often prove to be unreliable, detailed observation is a plus: observing what the current situation is, independent of the prevailing culture or customs. This talent of highly sensitive people can provide a good balance.

Subtle observation is also important in order to maintain our living environment. Both in terms of nature and in the figurative living environment, the atmosphere. Highly sensitive people are the first to suffer from a 'toxic' environment. They are strongly influenced by their environment. If they can perceive at an early stage that it is becoming unhealthy/toxic, action can be taken in time. If their signals are dismissed as exaggeration, because no one else perceives the change (in atmosphere) yet, intervention can come too late and the health of the entire group will suffer.

2. Talent to enjoy the little things

Perceiving all those stimuli is often seen as unfavorable. However, that is not the whole story. On the one hand, this profound perception often leads to overstimulation and stress. On the other hand, highly sensitive people are also very receptive to positive emotions, especially when it concerns their loved ones. They can really derive pleasure from the 'normal' things such as enjoying a cup of tea with a loved one in the sun. Or a butterfly sitting on a flower. This is a particularly enjoyable talent for the highly sensitive person himself. It makes it relatively easy for him to replenish his energy. But it can also be important for society. For example, in professions where creating a pleasant atmosphere is important, this can be a highly useful talent. Moreover, it counterbalances the materialistic tendency to derive happiness from possessions.

3. Talent to understand the other's perspective

Highly sensitive people have a great capacity to empathize. Their brain automatically tunes in to the feelings and perspectives of others. Everyone longs for understanding and connection, yet, within our society, we are increasingly focused on efficiency. In healthcare, for example, a lot of cutbacks have been made in recent decades. The practices are covered financially, but intangible matters such as attention are not. While various studies indicate how important this aspect of care is. Psychological well-being has a major effect on health. In addition, more and more people feel lonely, both the elderly as well as the young. Investing in people who can give real attention, the highly sensitive employees, will undoubtedly save a lot of costs and have a major effect on the well-being of the people who need care.

Highly sensitive people process information in depth. They have a strong pause-to-check system: the tendency to observe in a new situation before taking action. HSPs consider how the information relates to previous observations (number 2 in figure 11.1) and there is a strong coordination between brain and body (number 3). Three talents are related to this.

4. Talent to see the bigger picture

If you react directly to the situation you are in, you will not have time to look at how that situation relates to the big picture. Due to the information processing strategy of the highly sensitive brain, this consideration does take place in highly sensitive people. They need some time to place the new information in relation to what is already known, but are subsequently very capable of identifying connections. Connections that are sometimes overlooked by others. This is related to the following talent.

5. Talent to make well-considered decisions

In a society where quick decisions are the norm, the value of deliberation has been pushed to the background. In her book *Quiet,* Susan Cain shows that extroverts quickly work towards their goal and this activity makes it seem like they are performing better. But studies where test subjects have to complete more complicated assignments show that the people who think more carefully and persevere, even when it is difficult, perform much better. She argues that the bank crisis could have even been avoided if the preference had not consistently been given to quick, risky, short-term decisions.

Highly sensitive people are good at identifying cohesion and mapping out pros and cons. They oversee the risks of a (future) situation and do not merely look at the current situation, but also at what could happen (number 4 in figure 11.1). The advantage of this is that they identify risks in time and can therefore take them into account. Therefore, in my opinion, a good balance between decisiveness and deliberation is important within a team.

6. Talent to make intuitive decisions

Highly sensitive people have a strong intuition. This is related to a more sensitive interoception, the sense that perceives sensations from your body (number 3 in Figure 11-1). Research has shown that people with accurate interoception score better on intuitive decision-making. If you are more sensitive to sensations in the body, you can include that information in your decision making. Although we think that we mainly make rational decisions, most decisions are made unconsciously. It is therefore a great advantage if you have access to this 'unconscious' source of information. Another advantage is that highly sensitive people are also better able to regulate their body. If this talent is undeveloped, signals are ignored or you do not know how to deal with it. When this talent is developed, it becomes an important instrument in calming the stress system. And thus promotes intuitive decision-making.

The optimal-option-ambition plays a major role during the in-depth processing. The highly sensitive brain is strongly focused on the social context: on its own position in the group, but especially on the interests of others and the group as a whole (number 5 in figure 11.1). The highly sensitive brain always uses the entire toolbox, when approaching social as well as substantive issues. Three talents arise from this.

7. Talent to read the social context

What do I want? How can I achieve a successful career as soon as possible? What is good for me? These questions seem to drive the average employee. Yet we still need the group to survive. Our brain is geared to that. We want to be part of the group. The highly sensitive brain is even more focused on this. It performs a social check almost by default. How will my action be perceived in the social group; does it lead to reward or rejection? What are the interests of the group? The great capacity to empathize of highly sensitive people is closely related to this.

Elke Geraerts describes how important social talent is in her book *Het nieuwe mental* (The new mind). She writes that mankind's success does not come from his intellectual ingenuity, but from the ability to build and maintain social networks.[4] Because we are social by nature, we have been able to develop our intellect. This is also known as the social intelligence hypothesis: due to the evolutionary pressure to become socially smarter, our brain has changed, making us more intelligent in non-social areas as well. In that perspective, the growth of our brain is mainly explained by the increase of our social network.

We do not have to deny the value of an individualistic society to see how many benefits a supportive social group has. In fact, social support is seen as an important protective factor against burnouts.[5] Attention for the group as a whole and the survival of the group are therefore essential. In this, the ability of highly sensitive people to read the social context is of great importance.

8. Talent to take responsibility

Because highly sensitive people can read the social context well and are aware of the interests of the group as a whole, they have a great sense of responsibility. When a certain task is not performed, they take it on. If a project is compromised, they will naturally go the extra mile to fix it. I say 'naturally' because they may have unlearned this behavior over the years. Additionally, highly sensitive people often have a great sense of social awareness. They oversee the consequences of decision-making and are therefore concerned about the climate, poverty, animal suffering, et cetera. They are also willing to contribute to solutions. This social involvement is under pressure. It seems to be increasingly exceptional to commit oneself (voluntarily) to something. This increases the pressure on volunteers, sometimes making it harder for people to perform their tasks. If you need people who take responsibility, then highly sensitive people are right for the task.

9. Talent to think creatively

Creativity arises when you make unexpected connections, when you are able to think outside the box and look at a problem and see its complexity independently of the 'fixed' procedures. Albert Einstein said, 'In the middle of difficulty lies possibility.'

Highly sensitive people have a large reservoir of observations because they perceive in detail and combine these observations with new information. This enables them to perceive more complexity. From this complexity they can arrive at innovative insights (number 6 in figure 11.1).

In a society where we seem to be swayed by the issues of the day, this is an important quality. Many people flee when a problem seems too complex. They want a quick fix. Responding to these issues entails a quick response, which later turns out to be problematic as well, causing an emergency repair to be carried out. This creates a patchwork of solutions that often have very little to do with the purpose for which they were conceived. Instead of opting for a quick fix, the time could be taken to achieve creativity through complexity, to reach a better approach that brings us closer to the objective as well as preventing further problems.

The issues businesses and governments are facing today are often complex in nature. Simpler work has often been automated, making many positions heavily burdened. As a result, employees are increasingly expected to make their own decisions regarding complex issues. In doing so, creative thinking is a plus.

The final defining point of the highly sensitive brain is the ultimate response (number 7 in Figure 11.1). After the in-depth processing, both in terms of stress and emotions, this response is often more intense. That does not have to be a disadvantage, because both apply direction to action. The highly sensitive brain subsequently actively evaluates (number 8 in Figure 11.1). The tenth talent is connected to this.

10. Talent for self-reflection and improvement

The intense processing does not stop once an HSP has responded. After all, this reaction has created a new situation. The information from

that new situation is combined with the thought processes that preceded it. Furthermore, a highly sensitive person wonders whether he has done well and what could be improved. This strong self-reflection is an important motor for improvement and self-development.
In teams where people mainly work on a routine basis, this tenth talent is a nice addition. Where people are merely serving their time and do things simply because they have always been done this way, you need people who can look at themselves and are eager to improve. Who see the opportunities and the possibilities to do even better.

Symphony

By acknowledging and appreciating these talents and incorporating them into current working methods, I expect much more balance will arise. It is not my intention to present the highly sensitive method of information processing as an ideal. The talents of HSPs are no more valuable than other talents. But it is my deepest conviction that in society, we need all kinds of talents, because it is precisely the combination of them that creates a beautiful symphony.
At present, I sometimes have the feeling that only the brass players get the stage. Magnificent. But also very loud, shrill and monotonous. Therefore, I argue in favor of the inclusion of violins, flutes, and pianos in the symphony. The abovementioned talents of highly sensitive people can contribute to this more balanced interplay.

For highly sensitive people it will have great effect if they experience appreciation for their talents. Many HSPs have the feeling they have to adapt to the prevailing norms. Due to their great adaptive capacity, they come a long way in this. But because their brain works differently, it always leads to increased stress and misbudgeting of bodily resources. Appreciation of the natural talents of highly sensitive people will have the following effects:

- they feel more appreciated;
- they feel less socially rejected;

- they look at themselves with more acceptance and compassion;
- and therefore experience less stress;
- which will increase their performance;
- and their talents can be used optimally;
- from which the family, group, team or organization can benefit.

It's not a one-way street. Highly sensitive people themselves can contribute to acceptance by accepting themselves more. By seeing that what they might have always considered as a downside might be a talent. But also by demanding space to do 'their thing'. Just like Alanis Morissette, who found out that the result of her trait (those beautiful songs) cannot exist without the trait (high sensitivity) itself. Feel free to claim your alone time, cherish your intense emotions, allow yourself to see complexity in what others consider to be simple. Know that the highly sensitive brain uses these ingredients to achieve good results.

Sheet music

An important step in breaking through patterns is increasing our emotional literacy, building a larger emotion dictionary. This has two effects. First of all, we are better able to explain to the other what is going on inside us and what we need, so the other person has more tools to help us. And vice versa, we also understand the other better. In both situations, our mutual connection becomes stronger.

Secondly, high emotional literacy has a positive effect on our brain. The way we interpret experiences, the words we give to them, the brain sees as sheet music. Do we interpret a situation as (socially) threatening? Then the brain gives the order to activate the stress system. Do we see the (social) situation as rewarding? Then reward substances are released that make us feel good. The more precisely we interpret, the more precisely our brain can respond. A large emotion dictionary gives us the notes to write a beautiful symphony.

11.5 YOU SHOULD NOT ASK A FISH TO CLIMB A TREE

I started this book with a quote by Einstein
'Everybody is a genius. But if you judge a fish by its ability to climb a tree, it will live its whole life believing that it is stupid.'

This quote touches me. Perhaps because Albert Einstein was born on the same day as I, albeit almost a hundred years earlier. Maybe because it gives words to a feeling that I have known all my life. If you ask a fish to climb a tree, it will feel stupid, lacking, or like a failure. Anyone can climb a tree, why can't he?

Figure 11.2 Do not judge a fish by its ability to climb a tree

Because of its adaptability, the fish will still try to climb the tree. This activity is not natural to him and costs him a lot of energy, his bodily resources quickly depleted, and his stress system constantly activated. The issues he has as a result are then met with incomprehension. These do not resemble the issues others have in a similar situation and the solutions that work for others do not suit the fish at all. This reinforces his feeling that something is wrong with him.
If he listens to his intuition, he knows the proposed solutions are not useful to him. He knows that improving the quality of the water is crucial to him. But others see this as a waste of resources, after all, the water looks fine.

That water for swimming is the social environment for highly sensitive people. Due to their focus on the social context and their ability to sense the emotions of others, they are strongly influenced by the social setting. It may seem normal to others, but HSPs feel the subcutaneous tensions and the 'poison' it contains. This social stress quickly leads to chronic stress and thus a stronger focus on social threats, which increases the stress even further.
The social environment makes the difference between struggling and thriving. In a supportive setting, highly sensitive people appear to do much better than the average person. They benefit greatly from their sensitivity to the environment; they are able to use their talents and perform well.

One way to create those optimal conditions is to increase your emotion dictionary and approach yourself with compassion. In this way, you supply your brain with the instructions to respond appropriately. Moreover, you are better able to connect with others and maintain this connection better. Both tools prevent the self-reinforcing cycle of social rejection and help keep HSPs healthy.

If you ask a fish to do what it does best, it will flourish and the group will also benefit. With all its talents, it can see the threats and possibilities in a situation. The fish has a perfect sense of what the group needs. Through success experiences, it increasingly learns to trust its creative ideas. Its talents are appreciated and the fish feels that there is room to further develop its qualities and create optimal conditions for himself. That is why it excels. Society benefits because the qualities of the fish are fundamental for a good balance. This sense of meaning then gives the fish new energy to use its talents. It feels like a fish in water.

Endnotes

Introduction

1 Aron, 2005.
2 Cain, 2013.
3 Tol, 2014.
4 Aron, 2011.
5 According to Mascha Mooy, founder and owner of Bye Burnout, a burn-out costs up to € 122,000 per employee (Mooy, 2017).

Chapter 1 High Sensitivity

1 Aron and Aron, 1997.
2 Aron, 1996.
3 Aron and Aron, 1997.
4 Aron, Aron, and Jagiellowicz, 2012. In the first studies by Aron (Aron & Aron, 1997; Aron, 2004, 2005) the focus was on similarities and differences with the terms used up to that point, such as introversion, inhibition, shyness and emotionality. In later studies more attention was given to depth of processing.
5 Wolf, Van Doorn, and Weissing, 2008.
6 Aron, Aron, and Jagiellowicz, 2012. Lionetti, Aron, Aron, Burns, Jagiellowicz and Pluess (2018) speak of 31% among adults and Pluess, Assary, Lionetti, Lester, Krapohl, Aron and Aron (2017) about 20-35% in children.
7 Kagan, 1997.
8 Pluess and Belsky, 2010.
9 Aron et al., 2012.

10 Acevedo, Jagiellowicz, Aron, Marhenke, and Aron, 2017.
11 For an overview see Pluess, 2015b.
12 Melo and Anderson, 2015.
13 Licht, Mortensen, and Knudsen, 2011.
14 Homberg, Schubert, Asan, and Aron, 2016.
15 See also Pluess, 2015b.

Chapter 2 Highly Sensitive People

1 Bergsma, 2016. This includes some of my results regarding my research among adults. This research was replicated in English with 120 and in Spanish with 430 respondents. A report of the most recent study can be read in: Zegers de Beijl, 2019, Niños con alta sensibilidad, La Esfera de los Libros, Madrid.
2 Bergsma, 2016.
3 Bergsma, 2017.
4 Bergsma, 2019.
5 Bergsma, 2016.
6 Bergsma, 2016.
7 Bergsma, 2016.
8 Bergsma, 2019.

Chapter 3 The Brain

1 Godderis, 2015.
2 Zimbardo, Johnson, and McCan, 2013; Hersenstichting, n.d.; Ward, 2017; Cacioppo, Kalat and Freberg, 2018.
3 Maguire et al., 2003.
4 Janak and Tye, 2015.
5 Ward, 2017; Eisenberger, Lieberman, and Williams, 2003.
6 Bariselli, Glangetas, Tzanoulinou, and Bellone, 2016.
7 Ward, 2017.
8 Ward, 2017.
9 Ward, 2017.
10 Hersenstichting, n.d.
11 Palmer and Tsakiris, 2018.
12 Palmer and Tsakiris, 2018.
13 Wager and Barrett, 2017; Menon and Udin, 2010.
14 Menon and Udin, 2010.

15 Menon and Udin, 2010.
16 Menon and Udin, 2010.
17 Menon and Udin, 2010.
18 Buckner, 2012.
19 Feldman Barrett, 2017.
20 Raz et al., 2016.
21 Rizzolatti, Fadiga, Gallese, and Fogassi, 1996.
22 Ward, 2017; Woodruff and Stevens, 2018.
23 Cullen, Kanai, Bahrami, and Rees, 2014; Ward, 2017; Woodruff and Stevens, 2018.
24 Iacoboni, Molnar-Szakacs, Gallese, Bucciono, Mazziotta, en Rizzolatti, 2005.
25 Zaki and Ochsner, 2012.
26 Baron-Cohen, Lombardo, and Tager-Flusberg, 2013.
27 Ward, 2017.
28 Feldman Barrett, 2017.
29 Barrett and Satpute, 2013.
30 Feldman Barrett, 2017.
31 Mohan, De Ridder, and Vanneste, 2016.
32 Feldman Barrett, 2017.
33 Feldman Barrett, 2017.
34 *Voorpret* and *gezelligheid* are notoriously difficult words to translate to English. To illustrate, *Gezelligheid* has a Danish parallel of *Hygge*, which represents a similar warmth, though does not have the same social connotation.

Chapter 4 Visualizing the Highly Sensitive Brain

1 Longitudinal research is research where people are followed for a long period time.
2 Shaw et al., 2018.
3 Duan et al., 2018.
4 Batstra, 2014.

Chapter 5 Perception

1 Van Doorn, 2015.
2 Bergsma, 2016.
3 Bergsma, 2015.

4 Bergsma, 2016.
5 Bergsma, 2016.
6 Van Gijn, Bierman, Zuketto, and Rooijmans, 2000.
7 Bartoshuk and Snyder, 2016.
8 Dunn, 2007.
9 Lafer-Sousa, Hermann, and Conway, 2015.
10 Noticing sensory stimuli more strongly can also be part of disorders such as ASD and PTSD. Acevedo et al. (2018) conducted a review of brain studies and showed that some areas in SPS (high sensitivity), ASD, and PTSD are more strongly activated (the precentral gyrus, the caudate, the thalamo-cingulate circuit, and parts of the default mode network), but that SPS based on brain activation differs greatly from these disorders, due to the strong activation of the insula, the temporo-parietal junction, the ventral tegmental area. and the prefrontal cortex (among others).
11 Bergsma, 2016.
12 This term was coined by Daniel Goleman (2013).
13 Ward, 2017; Woodruff and Stevens, 2018.
14 Acevedo et al., 2014.
15 Acevedo et al., 2014.
16 Acevedo et al., 2017.
17 Acevedo et al., 2014. Research by Jagiellowicz (2012) and Acevedo et al. (2017) supports this.
18 Jagiellowicz, 2012.
19 Jagiellowicz, 2012.
20 Jagiellowicz, Aron, and Aron, 2016.
21 Jagiellowicz, Xu, Aron, Aron, Cao, Feng, and Weng, 2011.
22 The right claustrum, left occipitotemporal, bilateral temporal and medial and posterior parietal regions, and the right cerebellum (Jagiellowicz et al., 2011).
23 Gerstenberg, 2012.
24 Roiser, Rogers, Cook, and Sahakian, 2006.
25 Borg et al., 2009.

Chapter 6 Pause-to-check

1 Kagan, 1997.
2 McNaughton and Gray, 2000.
3 McNaughton and Gray, 2000.

4 Aron, Aron, and Jagiellowicz, 2012.
5 Aron et al., 2012.
6 Marvin Zuckerman (1979) introduced this term. He distinguishes four dimensions: Thrill and Adventure Seeking, Disinhibition, Experience Seeking, Boredom Susceptibility.
7 Acevedo et al., 2014.
8 Homberg, Schubert, Asan, and Aron, 2016.
9 Acevedo et al., 2014.
10 Acevedo et al., 2017.
11 Bergsma, 2016.
12 Bergsma, 2016.
13 Aron, Ketay, Hedden, Aron, Markus, and Gabrieli, 2010.
14 The frontal and parietal areas are more strongly activated when the problem is perceived as difficult.
15 Ceunen, Vlaeyen and Van Diest, 2016.
16 Kelly Mahler wrote this book on the subject in 2015: *Interoception: The eighth sensory system. Practical solutions for improving self-regulation, self-awareness and social understanding of individuals with autism spectrum and related disorders.*
17 Ceunen et.al., 2016.
18 Ceunen et.al., 2016.
19 Acevedo et al., 2014; Acevedo et al., 2017.
20 Acevedo et al., 2017.
21 Acevedo et al., 2014.i
22 Acevedo et al., 2017.
23 Jagiellowicz, 2012.
24 Acevedo et al., 2017.
25 Zie Ceunen et al., 2016.
26 Dunn et al., 2010.
27 Piech et al., 2017.
28 Wager, 2017.
29 The hypothalamus is part of the so-called HPA axis, which stimulates the production of cortisol via the hypothalamus, pituitary gland and adrenal glands. In addition, the hypothalamus steers the autonomic nervous system, which transfers adrenaline into the bloodstream via the adrenal glands. See chapter 3 and section 9.1.
30 Acevedo et al., 2017.

31 These activations are even more visible in highly sensitive people who experienced a good, supportive childhood (Acevedo et al., 2017).

Chapter 7 Optimal-option-ambition

1 He et al., 2010.
2 Bechara, Damásio, Damásio, and Anderson, 1994.
3 Knoch, Pascual-Leone, Meyer, Treyer, and Fehr, 2006.
4 Judging whether the action is fair takes place in the insula. The initiation of the fair action occurs in the dorsolateral prefrontal cortex (Ward, 2017).
5 Acevedo et al., 2014.
6 He et al., 2010.
7 Specifically, the dorsal region of the ACC (Ward, 2017).
8 Ward, 2017.
9 Jagiellowicz, 2012.
10 The ventral area processes affective and social stimuli regarding the question what these mean for belonging to the group (Ward, 2017).
11 In the case of positive images, this connection remained in force when corrected for childhood experiences. When compared to non-highly sensitive people, HSPs with a good and bad childhood thus have a more activated ACC when they look at images that evoke a positive emotion.
12 Ward, 2017.
13 Eisenberger et al., 2003.
14 Also see 6.3, Sensory integration
15 Williams and Sommer, 1997.
16 Zadro, Williams, and Richardson, 2004.
17 Van Beest and Williams, 2006.
18 Lieberman and Eisenberger, 2006.
19 Emotional response studies typically examine either only men or only women, because the responses differ between the sexes.
20 Acevedo et al., 2017.
21 Ward, 2017.
22 Greene and Seligman, 2016.
23 Acevedo et al., 2017.
24 Woodruff and Stevens, 2018.
25 Neff, 2004.

26 Acevedo et al., 2014; Acevedo et al., 2017.
27 Wager and Feldman Barrett, 2017; Menon and Udin, 2010.
28 Woodruff and Stevens, 2018.
29 Baron-Cohen et al., 2013; Woodruff and Stevens, 2018.
30 In affective empathy, activation mainly occurs in the mPFC, insula and ACC (Woodruff and Stevens, 2018).
31 Woodruff and Stevens, 2018.
32 Frith, 2001.
33 Acevedo et al., 2017.
34 Acevedo et al., 2014.
35 Acevedo et al., 2017.
36 Acevedo et al., 2017. And this effect was even stronger for HSPs who experienced a good childhood.
37 Ruby and Decety, 2004.
38 Bernhardt and Singer, 2012; Woodruff and Stevens, 2018.
39 Acevedo et al., 2014.
40 Dietrich and Haider, 2017.
41 Dietrich and Haider, 2017. Also see Beaty, Benedek, Silvia, and Schacter, 2016.
42 Acevedo et al., 2017 respectively Acevedo et al., 2014.
43 Respectively Jagiellowicz et al., 2011 and Aron et al., 2010.
44 Volf, Kulikov, Bortsov, and Popova, 2009.
45 The angular gyrus is located in the parietal lobe, which is involved in experiencing motor and sensory sensations. This area is also known as Brodman area 39.
46 Ramachandran and Hubbard, 2003.
47 Acevedo et al., 2014.
48 Pick and Lavidor, 2017.
49 Bergsma, 2016 and see chapter 2.
50 Acevedo et al., 2014.
51 Carson, Peterson, and Higgins, 2003.

Chapter 8 Reacting

1 Jagiellowicz et al., 2016.
2 Aron, Aron and Davies, 2005.
3 Lerner, Li, Valdesolo, and Kassam, 2015.
4 Boyce, 2019.

5 Boyce, 2019.

6 The functioning of oxytocine is broader. Among other things, it is involved in the orgasm, child birth, breast feeding, and parenting style. See Carter, 2014.

7 Rodrigues, Saslow, Garcia, John, and Keltner, 2009.

8 Ward, 2017.

9 Pluess, 2015b.

10 Sturge-Apple, Cicchettie, Davies, and Suor, 2012.

11 Pluess, 2017.

12 Pluess and Boniwell, 2015.

13 Eley et al., 2012.

14 Eley et al., 2012.

15 Aron and Aron, 1997.

16 Boyce, 2019.

17 Aron, 2005.

18 VTA/SN, caudal cingulate, hippocampus, hypothalamus, PAG, medial prefrontal cortex, right ACC, FG, TPJ, STG/MTG, left caudate tail, insula, IFG, parietal area, ITG and prefrontal cortex. Most areas are also more strongly activated in HSPs in general. Unique for HSPs with a good childhood are: left VTA, IFG, and right hypothalamus (Acevedo et al., 2017).

19 Acevedo et al., 2017; Acevedo et al., 2014.

20 Acevedo et al., 2017.

21 Acevedo et al., 2017.

22 Bariselli, Glangetas, Tzanoulinou, and Bellone, 2016.

23 The ventral striatum learns the emotional value of an action, and links emotion to reward and action. Consider, for example, the situation where you feel happy due to the attention you receive after doing something kind or rather something inapropriate. The area has connections to the amygdala, hippocampus, and anterior cingulate cortex (ACC), as well as to the orbifrontal cortex. The OFC determines how rewarding a stimulus is at the moment. When eating chocolate, for example, the reward is initially high, but that feeling of reward decreases when a lot has been eaten. At that point, the stimulus chocolate is no longer as rewarding. This shift can be observed in the OFC (Ward, 2017).

24 Bartels and Zeki, 2004.

25 Acevedo et al., 2017.

26 Moutsiana, Fearon, Murray, Cooper, Goodyer, Johnstone, and Halligan, 2014.

27 Acevedo et al., 2014. Research by Canli (2006) shows that a happy face is more rewarding for extroverts. Although the majority of highly sensitive people are introverted, they also experience more reward, but only when it comes to the happy face of their partner.

28 Both amygdala, hippocampus, parietal area, temporal pole, MFG, ventromedial prefrontal cortex, dorsomedial prefrontal cortex, SII, SMA, left hypothalamus, PC, TPJ, sensorimotor cortex, right STG, MTG, ITG, FG, precentral gyrus, frontal pole. Most areas overlap with HSP and negative images in general. Unique for HSP with good childhood: no deactivation of VTA and caudate and IFG. Stronger activation of the dorsomedial prefrontal context, FG, precentral gyrus, frontal pole, and sensorimotor cortex (Acevedo et al., 2017).

29 But only in these situations. In general, the amygdala of highly sensitive people is activated just as strongly as that of non-highly sensitive people. (Acevedo et al., 2017).

30 This brain area is connected to the so-called *commun humanity*, one of the three pillars of self-compassion according to Neff (2004).

31 Acevedo et al., 2017.

Chapter 9 Stress, the Brain, and Emotional Literacy

1 Fink, 2016.

2 Fink, 2016.

3 Radley, Morilak, Viau, and Campeau, 2015.

4 Schmaal et al., 2016.

5 Frodl et al., 2006.

6 Petrova, 2015.

7 Feldman Barrett, 2017.

8 DeAngelis, 2002.

9 Feldman Barrett, 2017.

10 Arkowitz and Lilienfeld, 2010.

11 Acevedo et al., 2017.

12 Feldman Barrett, 2017.

13 Feldman Barrett, 2017.

14 In addition, there were more differences found. The empathy areas (insula, inferior frontal gyrus, temporo-parietal junction), the prefron-

tral cortex, the hippocampus, hypothalamus and amygdala were, for example, strongly activated in highly sensitive people and less in people with autism (Acevedo et al., 2018).

15 Schaufeli and Bakker, 2007.
16 Feldman Barrett, 2017.
17 Kircanski et al., 2012.
18 Boyce, 2019.
19 Feldman Barrett, 2017.

Chapter 10 Social Rejection and Self-compassion

1 Taylor, Klien, Lewis, Gruenewald, Gurung, and Updegraff, 2000.
2 Taylor, 2011.
3 In difficult situations, women also seek more social support as a way of dealing with the situation. They are more, but not soley, focused on good connections within the group than men are. (Tamres, Janicki & Helgeson, 2002).
4 Greene and Seligman, 2016.
5 Shamay-Tsoory and Abu-Akel, 2016.
6 Boyce, 2019.
7 Stress has an effect on memory, as I wrote in Chapter 9. Prolonged stress shrinks the hippocampus and enlarges the amygdala. This makes it more difficult to bring factual and contextual information to the surface, the events are mainly given an emotional coloring.
8 Kirschbaum, Pirke, and Hellhammer, 1993.
9 Dickerson, Gable, Irwin, Aziz, and Kemeny, 2009.
10 Slavich, Way, Eisenberger, and Taylor, 2010.
11 Slavich et al., 2010.
12 Inagaki et al., 2015.
13 Eisenberger, Moieni, Inagaki, Muscatell, and Irwin, 2017.
14 Eisenberger et al., 2017.
15 Downey and Feldman, 1996.
16 Ayduk, Downey, and Kim, 2001.
17 Bakermans-Kranenburg and Van IJzendoorn, 2009.
18 Aron and Aron, 1997.
19 From research by Boyce (2019), Pluess (2015) and Belsky (2005). See also the box in chapter 1.
20 Groh, Narayan, Bakermans-Kranenburg, Roisman, Vaughn, Fearon, and Van IJzendoorn, 2017.

21 Moieni et al. (2015) made a composite metric for disconnection, consisting of loneliness, fearful attachment and rejection sensitivity. The score on that metric was linked to the increase in cytokines under stress: the more feeling of exclusion, the more inflammatory activity.
22 John-Henderson, Rheinschmidt, and Mendoza-Denton, 2015.
23 Bergsma, 2018.
24 Brené Brown wrote *I thought it was just me* (2007), *The gifts of imperfection* (2010), *Daring greatly* (2012), *Rising strong* (2015) and *Braving the wilderness* (2017) regarding her findings in the field of shame, courage, vulnerability, and empathy.
25 Boyce, 2019.
26 Warren, Smeets, and Neff, 2016.
27 Warren et al., 2016.
28 Brown, 2018.

Chapter 11 Recognizing and Acknowledging Talents

1 Wolf et al., 2008.
2 DeWulf, 2012.
3 These steps are central in the so-called Z quadrant for high sensitivity which I developed to reconnect high sensitive people with themselves (Bergsma, 2016).
4 Geraerts, 2016.
5 Schaufeli and Bakker, 2007.

Bibliography

Acevedo, B. P., Aron, E. N., Aron, A., Sangster, M.-D., Collins, N., & Brown, L. L. (2014). The highly sensitive brain: an fMRI study of sensory processing sensitivity and response to others' emotions. *Brain Behav*, 4: 580–594. doi:10.1002/brb3.242

Acevedo, B. P., Jagiellowicz, J., Aron, E., Marhenke, R., & Aron, A. (2017). Sensory processing sensitivity and childhood quality's effects on neural responses to emotional stimuli. *Clinical Neuropsychiatry*, (6), p359-373.

Acevedo, B., Aron, E., Pospos, S., & Jessen, D. (2018). The functional highly sensitive brain: a review of the brain circuits underlying sensory processing sensitivity and seemingly related disorders. *Philosophical Transactions of the Royal Society B: Biological Sciences*, 373(1744), 20170161.

Arkowitz, H., & Lilienfeld, S. O. (2010). Why science tells us not to rely on eyewitness accounts. *Scientific American, Jan, 1.*

Aron, E. N. (1996). *The highly sensitive person: How to thrive when the world overwhelms you.* New York, Birch Lane Press.

Aron, E. N., & Aron, A. (1997). Sensory-processing sensitivity and its relation to introversion and emotionality. *Journal of Personality and Social Psychology*, 73, 345–368.

Aron, E. (2004), Revisiting Jung's concept of innate sensitiveness. *Journal of Analytical Psychology*, 49, 337-367.

Aron, E. (2005). *Het werkboek voor Hoog Sensitieve Personen.* Archipel: Amsterdam.

Aron, E., Aron, A., & Davies, K.M. (2005). Adult shyness: the interaction of temperamental sensitivity and an adverse childhood environment. *Personality and Social Psychology Bulletin*, 31, 181-197.

Aron, A., Ketay, S., Hedden, R., Aron, E. N., Markus, H. R., & Gabrieli, J. D. E. (2010). Temperament trait of sensory processing sensitivity moderates cultural differences in neural response. *Social Cognitive and Affective Neuroscience*, 5, 219–226.

Aron, E. N. (2011). *Psychotherapy and the Highly Sensitive Person: Improving outcomes for that minority of people who are the majority of clients.* Routledge.

Aron, E.N., Aron, A., & Jagiellowicz, J. (2012). Sensory Processing Sensitivity: A review in the light of the Evolution of Biological Responsivity, *Personality and Social Psychology Review,* DOI: 10.1177/1088868311434213

Assary, E., & Pluess, M. (2017). Differential susceptibility in minority children: Individual differences in environmental sensitivity. In *Handbook on Positive Development of Minority Children and Youth* (pp. 139-152). Springer, Cham.

Ayduk, O., Downey, G., & Kim, M. (2001). Rejection sensitivity and depressive symptoms in women. *Personality and Social Psychology Bulletin, 27*(7), 868-877.

Bakermans-Kranenburg, M. J., & van IJzendoorn, M. H. (2009). The first 10,000 Adult Attachment Interviews: Distributions of adult attachment representations in clinical and non-clinical groups. *Attachment & human development, 11*(3), 223-263.

Bar-Haim, Y., Fox, N. A., Benson, B., Guyer, A. E., Williams, A., Nelson, E. E., Perez-Edgar, K., Pine, D. S., ... Ernst, M. (2009). Neural correlates of reward processing in adolescents with a history of inhibited temperament. *Psychological science, 20*(8), 1009-18.

Bariselli, S., Glangetas, C., Tzanoulinou, S., & Bellone, C. (2016). Ventral tegmental area subcircuits process rewarding and aversive experiences. *Journal of neurochemistry*, 139(6), 1071-1080.

Barrett, L. F., & Satpute, A. B. (2013). Large-scale brain networks in affective and social neuroscience: towards an integrative functional architecture of the brain. *Current opinion in neurobiology, 23*(3), 361-372.

Bartels, A., & Zeki, S. (2004). The neural correlates of maternal and romantic love. *Neuroimage*, 21(3), 1155-1166.

Bartoshuk, L. M., & Snyder, D. J. (2016). Taste. *Neuroscience in the 21st Century: From Basic to Clinical*, 903-934.

Baron-Cohen, Simon, Michael Lombardo & Helen Tager-Flusberg (eds.) (2013). *Understanding Other Minds: Perspectives From Developmental Social Neuroscience.* Oxford University Press.

Batstra, L., Nieweg, E. H., & Hadders-Algra, M. (2014). Exploring five common assumptions on Attention Deficit Hyperactivity Disorder. *Acta Paediatrica, 103*(7), 696-700.

Beaty, R. E., Benedek, M., Silvia, P. J., & Schacter, D. L. (2016). Creative cognition and brain network dynamics. *Trends in cognitive sciences, 20*(2), 87-95.

Bechara, A., Damásio, A. R., Damásio, H., & Anderson, S. W. (1994). 'Insensitivity to future consequences following damage to human prefrontal cortex'. *Cognition*. 50 (1–3): 7–15. doi:10.1016/0010-0277(94)90018-3

Beest, I. van, & Williams, K (2006). 'When inclusion costs and ostracism pays, ostracism still hurts'. *Journal of Personality and Social Psychology*. 42 (2): 213–220

Belsky, J. (2005). Differential susceptibility to rearing influence. *Origins of the social mind: Evolutionary psychology and child development,* 139-163.

Bergsma, E.N. (2015). Counselling bij hoogsensitiviteit, *Counselling Magazine,* nr. 4.

Bergsma, E.N. (2016). *Hoogsensitieve kinderen, praktische leidraad voor ouders en professionals,* Booklight.

Bergsma, E.N. (2019), Overwhelmed. From: https://hoogsensitief.nl/overwhelmed-hsp-notice-more-subtleties/

Bergsma, E.N. (2019). *Effects of being overwhelmed.* From: https://hoogsensitief.nl/effects-of-being-overwhelmed/

Bernhardt, B. C., & Singer, T. (2012). The Neural Basis of Empathy. *Annu. Rev. Neurosci,* 35, 1-23.

Borg, J., Henningsson, S., Saijo, T., Inoue, M., Bah, J., Westberg, L.,... & Halldin, C. (2009). Serotonin transporter genotype is associated with cognitive performance but not regional 5-HT1A receptor binding in humans. *International Journal of Neuropsychopharmacology, 12*(6), 783-792.

Bos, R. van den, Homberg, J., & de Visser, L. (2013). A critical review of sex differences in decision-making tasks: Focus on the Iowa Gambling Task. *Behavioural Brain Research, 238,* 95-108.

Bosch, I. (2011). *PRI en de kunst van bewust leven.* Atlas Contact.

Boyce, T. (2019). *The Orchid and the Dandelion. Why some people struggle and how all can thrive.* Bluebird.

Boyce, W. T., & Ellis, B. J. (2005). Biological sensitivity to context: I. An evolutionary–developmental theory of the origins and functions of stress reactivity. *Development and psychopathology, 17*(2), 271-301.

Brown, B. (2018). *Dare to Lead. Brave Work. Tough Conversations. Whole Hearts.* Penguin, London.

Buchanan, T. & S. Preston (2016). When Feeling and Doing Diverge. In: Greene, J. D., & Seligman, M. E. (Eds.). (2016). *Positive neuroscience.* Oxford University Press.

Buckner RL (2012). The serendipitous discovery of the brain's default network. *NeuroImage,* 62: 1137-45.

Cacioppo, Kalat, & Freberg (2019). *Brain and behavior* Cengage Learning.

Cain, S. (2013). *Quiet: The power of introverts in a world that can't stop talking.* Broadway Books.

Canli, T. (Ed.). (2006). *Biology of personality and individual differences.* Guilford Press.

Carson, S. H., Peterson, J. B., & Higgins, D. M. (2003). Decreased latent inhibition is associated with increased creative achievement in high-functioning individuals. *Journal of Personality and Social Psychology, 85*(3), 499.

Carter, C. S. (2014). Oxytocin pathways and the evolution of human behavior. *Annual review of psychology, 65,* 17-39.

Ceunen, E., Vlaeyen, J. W., & Van Diest, I. (2016). On the origin of interoception. *Frontiers in psychology,* 7, 743.

Chen, C., Chen, C., Moyzis, R., Stern, H., He, Q., Li, H.,... & Dong, Q. (2011). Contributions of dopamine-related genes and environmental factors to highly sensitive personality: a multi-step neuronal system-level approach. *PloS one,* 6(7), e21636.

Conley, D., Rauscher, E., & Siegal, M. L. (2013). Beyond orchids and dandelions: Testing the 5-HTT 'risky' allele for evidence of phenotypic capacitance and frequency-dependent selection. *Biodemography and social biology, 59*(1), 37-56.

Coutinho, J. F., Silva, P. O., & Decety, J. (2014). Neurosciences, empathy, and healthy interpersonal relationships: Recent findings and implications for counseling psychology. *Journal of Counseling Psychology, 61*(4), 541.

Cullen, H., Kanai, R., Bahrami, B., & Rees, G., (2014). Individual differences in anthropomorphic attributions and human brain structure. *Social Cognitive and Affective Neuroscience,* 9(9), 1276-1280.

DeAngelis, T. (2002). A bright future for PNI. *Monitor on Psychology, 33*(6), 46-50.

Dewulf, L. (2012). *Ik kies voor mijn talent: wat is talent? Hoe talent ontwikkelen? En wat met waar je echt niet goed in bent?.* Lannoo Meulenhoff-Belgium.

Dickerson, S. S., Gable, S. L., Irwin, M. R., Aziz, N., & Kemeny, M. E. (2009). Social-evaluative threat and proinflammatory cytokine regulation: An experimental laboratory investigation. *Psychological Science, 20*(10), 1237-1244.

Dietrich, A., & Haider, H. (2017). A neurocognitive framework for human creative thought. *Frontiers in psychology*, 7, 2078.

Doorn, E. van (2015, 5 maart). *The dress en eigenaar onthullen de ware kleur*. From: https://www.metronieuws.nl/lifestyle/mode/2015/03/thedress-en-eigenaar-onthullen-de-ware-kleur.

Downey, G., & Feldman, S. I. (1996). Implications of rejection sensitivity for intimate relationships. *Journal of Personality and Social Psychology, 70*(6), 1327.

Duan, K., Chen, J., Calhoun, V. D., Lin, D., Jiang, W., Franke, B.,... & Liu, J. (2018). Neural correlates of cognitive function and symptoms in attention-deficit/hyperactivity disorder in adults. *NeuroImage: Clinical, 19*, 374-383.

Dunn, B. D., Galton, H. C., Morgan, R., Evans, D., Oliver, C., Meyer, M.,... & Dalgleish, T. (2010). Listening to your heart: How interoception shapes emotion experience and intuitive decision making. *Psychological science, 21*(12), 1835-1844.

Dunn, W. (2007). Supporting Children to Participate Successfully in Everyday Life by Using Sensory-Processing Knowledge, *Infants & Young Children*, Vol. 20, No. 2, pp. 84–101.

Eisenberger, N. I., Lieberman, M. D., & Williams, K. D. (2003). Does rejection hurt? An fMRI study of social exclusion. *Science*, 302(5643), 290-292.

Eisenberger, N. I., Moieni, M., Inagaki, T. K., Muscatell, K. A., & Irwin, M. R. (2017). In sickness and in health: the co-regulation of inflammation and social behavior. *Neuropsychopharmacology, 42*(1), 242.

Eley, T. C., Hudson, J. L., Creswell, C., Tropeano, M., Lester, K. J., Cooper, P.,... & Uher, R. (2012). Therapygenetics: the 5HTTLPR and response to psychological therapy. *Molecular psychiatry, 17*(3), 236.

Ellis, B. J., Boyce, W. T., Belsky, J., Bakermans-Kranenburg, M. J., & Van IJzendoorn, M. H. (2011). Differential susceptibility to the environment: An evolutionary–neurodevelopmental theory. *Development and psychopathology, 23*(1), 7-28.

Feldman Barrett, Lisa (2017). *How emotions are made. The secret life of the brain.* Boston. Houghton Mifflin Harcourt.

Fink, G. (Ed.). (2016). *Stress: Concepts, Cognition, Emotion, and Behavior: Handbook of Stress Series* (Vol. 1). Academic Press.

Frith, U. (2001). Mind blindness and the brain in autism. *Neuron, 32*(6), 969-979.

Frodl, T., Schaub, A., Banac, S., Charypar, M., Jäger, M., Kümmler, P.,... & Reiser, M. (2006). Reduced hippocampal volume correlates with executive dysfunctioning in major depression. *Journal of Psychiatry and Neuroscience,* 31(5), 316.

Geraerts, E. (2016). *Het nieuwe mentaal.* Lannoo.

Gerstenberg, F. X. (2012). Sensory-processing sensitivity predicts performance on a visual search task followed by an increase in perceived stress. *Personality and Individual Differences,* 53(4), 496-500.

Gijn J van, Bierman WFW, Zuketto C, & Rooijmans HGM (2000).Chronische, onverklaarde pijn: van klacht naar doel. *Ned Tijdschrift Geneeskunde*; 144:641-4.

Godderis, J. (2005). *De Hippocratische geneeskunde in al haar staten: reflecties over gezondheid en ziekte onder 't zachte fluisteren van de plataan.* Garant.

Goldstein, B., J. van Hooff, Kalat, J., Cacioppo, J., & Freberg, L. (2018), *Brain and Cognition,* Cengage learning.

Goleman, Daniel (2013). *Het brein en emotionele intelligentie,* Business Contact, Amsterdam.

Greene, J. D., & Seligman, M. E. (Eds.). (2016). *Positive neuroscience.* Oxford University Press.

Gray, J. (1985). Issues in the neuropsychology of anxiety. In: Ruma en Maser (red), *Anxiety and disorder* (pp 5-25). Hillsdale, NJ: Erlbaum.

Groh, A. M., Narayan, A. J., Bakermans-Kranenburg, M. J., Roisman, G. I., Vaughn, B. E., Fearon, R. P., & van IJzendoorn, M. H. (2017). Attachment and temperament in the early life course: A meta-analytic review. *Child development, 88*(3), 770-795.

Gyurak, A., Haase, C. M., Sze, J., Goodkind, M. S., Coppola, G., Lane, J.,... & Levenson, R. W. (2013). The effect of the serotonin transporter polymorphism (5-HTTLPR) on empathic and self-conscious emotional reactivity. *Emotion, 13*(1), 25.

He, Q., Xue, G., Chen, C., Lu, Z., Dong, Q., Lei, X.,... & Li, J. (2010). Serotonin transporter gene-linked polymorphic region (5-HTTLPR) influences decision making under ambiguity and risk in a large Chinese sample. *Neuropharmacology,* 59(6), 518-526.

Hersenstichting (zd). Alles over hersenen. From: https://www.hersenstichting.nl/alles-over-hersenen.

Holzer, P. (2017). Interoception and gut feelings: unconscious body signals' impact on brain function, behavior and belief processes. In *Processes of believing: The acquisition, maintenance, and change in creditions* (pp. 435-442). Springer, Cham.

Homberg, J. R., Schubert, D., Asan, E., & Aron, E. N. (2016). Sensory processing sensitivity and serotonin gene variance: Insights into mechanisms shaping environmental sensitivity. *Neuroscience & Biobehavioral Reviews, 71,* 472-483.

Hoogendijk, W. en De Rek, W. (2017). *Van big bang tot burn-out.* Balans, Amsterdam.

Iacoboni, M., Molnar-Szakacs, I., Gallese, V., Buccino, G., Mazziotta, J. C., & Rizzolatti, G. (2005). Grasping the intentions of others with one's own mirror neuron system. *PLoS biology, 3*(3), e79. Inagaki, T. K., Muscatell, K. A., Irwin, M. R., Moieni, M., Dutcher, J. M., Jevtic, I.,... & Eisenberger, N. I. (2015). The role of the ventral striatum in inflammatory-induced approach toward support figures. *Brain, behavior, and immunity, 44,* 247-252.

Jagiellowicz, J., Xu, X., Aron, A, Aron, E. Cao, G., Feng, T., & Weng, X. (2011). The trait of sensory processing sensitivity and neural responses to changes in visual scenes, In: Social Cognitive and *Affective Neuroscience,* 6(1):38-47.

Jagiellowicz, J. (2012). *The relationship between the temperament trait of sensory processing sensitivity and emotional reactivity.* Doctoral Dissertation at Stony Brook University, New York.

Jagiellowicz, J., Aron, A., & Aron, E. N. (2016). Relationship between the temperament trait of sensory processing sensitivity and emotional reactivity. *Social Behavior and Personality: an international journal, 44*(2), 185-199.

Janak, P. H., & Tye, K. M. (2015). From circuits to behaviour in the amygdala. *Nature, 517*(7534), 284.

John-Henderson, N. A., Rheinschmidt, M. L., & Mendoza-Denton, R. (2015). Cytokine responses and math performance: The role of stereotype threat and anxiety reappraisals. *Journal of Experimental Social Psychology, 56,* 203-206.

Kagan, J. (1997), Temperament and the Reactions to Unfamiliarity, *Child Development,* February 1997, Volume 68, Number 1, Pages 139-143.

Kamerling, L. & Zunderdorp, L. (2018). *Overprikkeld. Eerste hulp bij hoogsensitiviteit.* Kosmos, Utrecht.

Kim, M. J., Loucks, R. A., Neta, M., Davis, F. C., Oler, J. A., Mazzulla, E. C., & Whalen, P. J. (2010). Behind the mask: the influence of mask-type on amygdala response to fearful faces. *Social cognitive and affective neuroscience, 5*(4), 363-368.

Kircanski, K., Lieberman, M. D., & Craske, M. G. (2012). Feelings into words: contributions of language to exposure therapy. *Psychological science, 23*(10), 1086-1091.

Kirschbaum, C., Pirke, K. M., & Hellhammer, D. H. (1993). The 'Trier Social Stress Test'—a tool for investigating psychobiological stress responses in a laboratory setting. Neuropsychobiology, 28(1-2), 76-81

Knoch, D., Pascual-Leone, A., Meyer, K., Treyer, V., & Fehr, E. (2006). Diminishing reciprocal fairness by disrupting the right prefrontal cortex. *science,* 314(5800), 829-832.

Lafer-Sousa, R., Hermann, K. L., & Conway, B. R. (2015). Striking individual differences in color perception uncovered by 'the dress' photograph. *Current Biology, 25*(13), R545-R546.

Lerner, J. S., Li, Y., Valdesolo, P., & Kassam, K. S. (2015). Emotion and decision making. *Annual review of psychology, 66.*

Licht, C. L., Mortensen, E. L., & Knudsen, G. M. (2011). Association between sensory processing sensitivity and the serotonin transporter polymorphism 5-HTTLPR short/short genotype. In *Biological Psychiatry* (Vol. 69, No. 9, pp. 152S-153S).

Lieberman, M. D., & Eisenberger, N. I. (2006). A pain by any other name (rejection, exclusion, ostracism) still hurts the same: The role of dorsal anterior cingulate cortex in social and physical pain. *Social neuroscience: People thinking about thinking people,* 167-187.

Lionetti, F., Aron, A., Aron, E. N., Burns, G. L., Jagiellowicz, J., & Pluess, M. (2018). Dandelions, tulips and orchids: evidence for the existence of low-sensitive, medium-sensitive and high-sensitive individuals. *Translational psychiatry, 8*(1), 24.

Maguire, E. A., Spiers, H. J., Good, C. D., Hartley, T., Frackowiak, R. S., & Burgess, N. (2003). Navigation expertise and the human hippocampus: a structural brain imaging analysis. *Hippocampus, 13*(2), 250-259.

Mah, L., Szabuniewicz, C., & Fiocco, A. J. (2016). Can anxiety damage the brain?. *Current opinion in psychiatry, 29*(1), 56-63.

McNaughton, N., & Gray, J. A. (2000). Anxiolytic action on the behavioural inhibition system implies multiple types of arousal contribute to anxiety. *Journal of affective disorders, 61*(3), 161-176.

Melo, H., & Anderson, A. (2015). Imaging genetics of positive psychology. In

Pluess, M. (Ed.). (2015). *Genetics of psychological well-being: the role of heritability and genetics in positive psychology*. Series in Positive Psychology.

Menon, V. en Uddin, L. (2010). Saliency, switching, attention and control: a network model of insula function, *Brain Struct Funct.*; 214(5-6): 655–667. doi:10.1007/s00429-010-0262-0.

Miller, E. K. (2000). The prefrontal cortex and cognitive control. Nature reviews. *Neuroscience*, 1(1), 59-65.

Miller, B. L., & Cummings, J. L. (Eds.). (2017). *The human frontal lobes: Functions and disorders*. Guilford Publications.

Mohan, A., De Ridder, D., & Vanneste, S. (2016). Emerging hubs in phantom perception connectomics. *NeuroImage: Clinical, 11*, 181-194.

Moieni, M., Irwin, M. R., Jevtic, I., Breen, E. C., Cho, H. J., Arevalo, J. M.,... & Eisenberger, N. I. (2015). Trait sensitivity to social disconnection enhances pro-inflammatory responses to a randomized controlled trial of endotoxin. *Psychoneuroendocrinology, 62*, 336-342.

Moore, S. R., & Depue, R. A. (2016). Neurobehavioral foundation of environmental reactivity. *Psychological bulletin, 142*(2), 107.

Mooy, M. (2017, 22 mei). *Jezelf lekker de afgrond in werken*. From: www.byebyeburnout.nl/jezelf-lekker-de-afgrond-in-werken/

Moutsiana, C., Fearon, P., Murray, L., Cooper, P., Goodyer, I., Johnstone, T., & Halligan, S. (2014). Making an effort to feel positive: insecure attachment in infancy predicts the neural underpinnings of emotion regulation in adulthood. *Journal of Child Psychology and Psychiatry*, 55(9), 999-1008.

Neff, K. D. (2004). Self-compassion and psychological well-being. *Constructivism in the Human Sciences*, 9, 27-37

Ofman, D. (2004). *Bezieling en kwaliteit in organisaties*. Servire, Kosmos, Utrecht.

Palmer, C. E., & Tsakiris, M. (2018). Going at the heart of social cognition: is there a role for interoception in self-other distinction?. *Current opinion in psychology*.

Petrova, S. (2015). *Depression damages part of the brain, research concludes*. From: https://theconversation.com/depression-damages-parts-of-the-brain-research-concludes-43915

Pick, H., & Lavidor, M. (2017). The role of the angular gyrus in creative and automatic tasks. *Clinical Neurophysiology, 128*(3), e97.

Piech, R. M., Strelchuk, D., Knights, J., Hjälmheden, J. V., Olofsson, J. K., & Aspell, J. E. (2017). People with higher interoceptive sensitivity are more altruistic, but improving interoception does not increase altruism. *Scientific reports*, 7(1), 15652.

Pluess, M., & Belsky, J. (2010). Differential susceptibility to parenting and quality child care. *Developmental psychology, 46*(2), 379.

Pluess, M. (2015a). Individual Differences in Environmental Sensitivity, *Child Development Perspectives,* 9, 138-143.

Pluess, M. (Ed.). (2015b). *Genetics of psychological well-being: the role of heritability and genetics in positive psychology.* Series in Positive Psychology.

Pluess, M., & Boniwell, I. (2015). Sensory-Processing Sensitivity predicts treatment response to a school-based depression prevention program, *Personality and Individual Differences* 82 (2015) 40–45. *DOI: 10.1016/j.paid.2015.03.011*

Pluess, M., Assary, E., Lionetti, F., Lester, K. J., Krapohl, E., Aron, E. N., & Aron, A. (2018). Environmental sensitivity in children: Development of the Highly Sensitive Child Scale and identification of sensitivity groups. *Developmental psychology, 54*(1), 51.

Pluess, M. (2017). Vantage sensitivity: Environmental sensitivity to positive experiences as a function of genetic differences. *Journal of personality,* 85(1), 38-50.

Radley, J., Morilak, D., Viau, V., & Campeau, S. (2015). Chronic stress and brain plasticity: mechanisms underlying adaptive and maladaptive changes and implications for stress-related CNS disorders. *Neuroscience & Biobehavioral Reviews,* 58, 79-91.

Ramachandran, V.S., & Hubbard, E.M (2003). 'The Phenomenology of Synaesthesia'. *Journal of Consciousness Studies. 10* (8): 49–57.

Raz, G., Touroutoglou, A., Wilson-Mendenhall, C., Gilam, G., Lin, T., Gonen, T.,... & Maron-Katz, A. (2016). Functional connectivity dynamics during film viewing reveal common networks for different emotional experiences. *Cognitive, Affective, & Behavioral Neuroscience, 16*(4), 709-723.

Rizzolatti, G., Fadiga, L., Gallese, V., & Fogassi, L. (1996). Premotor cortex and the recognition of motor actions. *Cognitive brain research, 3*(2), 131-141.

Rodrigues, S. M., Saslow, L. R., Garcia, N., John, O. P., & Keltner, D. (2009). Oxytocin receptor genetic variation relates to empathy and stress reactivity in humans. *Proceedings of the National Academy of Sciences, 106*(50), 21437-21441.

Roiser, J. P., Rogers, R. D., Cook, L. J., & Sahakian, B. J. (2006). The effect of polymorphism at the serotonin transporter gene on decision-making, memory and executive function in ecstasy users and controls. *Psychopharmacology, 188*(2), 213-227.

Ruby, P., & Decety, J. (2004). How would you feel versus how do you think she would feel? A neuroimaging study of perspective-taking with social emotions. *Journal of cognitive neuroscience*, 16(6), 988-999.

Schaufeli, W., & Bakker, A. (Eds.). (2007). *De psychologie van arbeid en gezondheid.* Bohn Stafleu van Loghum.

Schoebi, D., Perrez, M., & Bradbury, T. N. (2012). Expectancy effects on marital interaction: Rejection sensitivity as a critical moderator. *Journal of Family Psychology, 26*(5), 709.

Schmaal, L., Veltman, D. J., van Erp, T. G., Sämann, P. G., Frodl, T., Jahanshad, N.,... & Vernooij, M. W. (2016). Subcortical brain alterations in major depressive disorder: findings from the ENIGMA Major Depressive Disorder working group. *Molecular psychiatry, 21*(6), 806.

Shamay-Tsoory, S. G., & Abu-Akel, A. (2016). The social salience hypothesis of oxytocin. *Biological psychiatry, 79*(3), 194-202.

Shaw, P., Ishii-Takahashi, A., Park, M. T., Devenyi, G. A., Zibman, C., Kasparek, S.,... & von Polier, G. (2018). A multicohort, longitudinal study of cerebellar development in attention deficit hyperactivity disorder. *Journal of Child Psychology and Psychiatry, 59*(10), 1114-1123.

Slavich, G. M., Way, B. M., Eisenberger, N. I., & Taylor, S. E. (2010). Neural sensitivity to social rejection is associated with inflammatory responses to social stress. *Proceedings of the National Academy of Sciences*, 201009164.

Sturge-Apple, M. L., Cicchetti, D., Davies, P. T., & Suor, J. H. (2012). Differential susceptibility in spillover between interparental conflict and maternal parenting practices: Evidence for OXTR and 5-HTT genes. *Journal of Family Psychology, 26*(3), 431.

Tamres, L. K., Janicki, D., & Helgeson, V. S. (2002). Sex differences in coping behavior: A meta-analytic review and an examination of relative coping. *Personality and Social Psychology review, 6*(1), 2-30.

Taylor, S. E., Klein, L. C., Lewis, B. P., Gruenewald, T. L., Gurung, R. A., & Updegraff, J. A. (2000). Biobehavioral responses to stress in females: tend-and-befriend, not fight-or-flight. *Psychological review, 107*(3), 411.

Taylor, S. E. (2011). Tend and befriend theory. *Handbook of Theories of Social Psychology: Collection: Volumes 1 & 2*, 32.

Tol, A. (2014). *Hoogsensitiviteit professioneel gezien. Sensitiviteit als verklaring onder psych(osomat)ische klachten*, Boom, Amsterdam.

Volf, N. V., Kulikov, A. V., Bortsov, C. U., & Popova, N. K. (2009). Association of verbal and figural creative achievement with polymorphism in the human serotonin transporter gene. *Neuroscience letters, 463*(2), 154-157.

Wager, T.D., & Feldman Barrett, L. (2017). From affect to control: functional specialization of the insula in motivation and regulation, *bioRxiv*, DOI: http://dx.DOI.org/10.1101/102368.

Ward, J. (2017). *The Student's Guide to Social Neuroscience,* Routledge, London.

Warren, R., Smeets, E., & Neff, K. (2016). 'Self-criticism and self-compassion: risk and resilience: being compassionate to oneself is associated with emotional resilience and psychological well-being.' *Current Psychiatry*, vol. 15, no. 12, 2016, p. 18-28.

Watt-Smith, T. (2016). *The Book of Human Emotions*. Profile Books Limited.

Williams, K. D., & Sommer, K. L. (1997). 'Social ostracism by one's coworkers: Does rejection lead to loafing or compensation?'. *Personality and Social Psychology Bulletin. 23* (7): 693–706.

Wimmer, H., & Perner, J. (1983). Beliefs about beliefs: Representation and constraining function of wrong beliefs in young children's understanding of deception. *Cognition, 13*(1), 103-128.

Woodruff, C. C., & Stevens, L. (2018). Where Caring for Self and Others Lives in the Brain, and How It Can Be Enhanced and Diminished: Observations on the Neuroscience of Empathy, Compassion, and Self-Compassion. In *The Neuroscience of Empathy, Compassion, and Self-Compassion* (pp. 285-320).

Wolf, M., Van Doorn, G. S., & Weissing, F. J. (2008). Evolutionary emergence of responsive and unresponsive personalities. *Proceedings of the National Academy of Sciences, 105*(41), 15825-15830.

Zadro, L., Williams, K., & Richardson, R. (2004). 'How low can you go? Ostracism by a computer is sufficient to lower self-reported levels of belonging, control, self-esteem and meaningful existence'. *Journal of Experimental Social Psychology. 40* (4): 560–567

Zaki, J. & Ochsner. K. (2012). The Neuroscience of Empathy: progress, pitfalls and promise, Nature *Neuroscience* volume 15, pages 675–680 (2012)

Zimbardo, Ph., R. Johnson, & V. McCann (2013). *Psychologie. Een inleiding.* Pearson Benelux.

Zimmer-Gembeck, M. J., Nesdale, D., Webb, H. J., Khatibi, M., & Downey, G. (2016). A longitudinal rejection sensitivity model of depression and aggression: Unique roles of anxiety, anger, blame, withdrawal and retribution. *Journal of abnormal child psychology, 44*(7), 1291-1307.

Keyword list

ACTH – This adrenocorticotropic hormone travels from the pituitary gland through the bloodstream to the adrenal gland. It produces cortisol. This hormone is of great importance in the HPA axis.

Adrenaline – A stress hormone that enables a person to fight or flee in a threatening situation.

Affect – Sensations in the body. Affect consists of two elements: valence (does it feel pleasant or unpleasant) and arousal (does it create tension or not).

Amygdala – Evaluates emotional information, both incoming sensory information and information from memory.

Angular gyrus (AG) – Brain area that is part of the cortex. Involved in processing language and understanding metaphors.

Anterior cingulate cortex (ACC) – 'Social Error Radar'; questioning whether you will be socially rewarded or punished for something. Active in (social) pain. Part of the cingulate cortex.

Basal ganglia – This area is important in movement and reward.

Behavioral activation system (BAS) – This is Gray's term to describe uninhibited behavior. The BAS is aimed at fulfilling needs and the urge to go for something.

Behavioral inhibition system (BIS) – This is Gray's term to describe inhibited behavior. The BIS produces alert attention and a pause in activity so that conflicting information can be processed.

Biological sensitivity to context (BSC) – This is a theory by Boyce and Ellis in which they describe that dandelion children experience little effect from their environment and orchid children are strongly influenced by the situation in which they grow up.

Brain Stem – This includes the medulla, the pons, and the thalamus. The brain stem is involved in vital body functions.

Central-executive network (CEN) – The brain regions of the central executive network are activated in cognitively demanding tasks.

Cerebellum – (literally 'small brains') – This area of the brain is involved in motion and maintaining balance.

Cerebral Cortex – This is the outermost layer of our brain directly under the skull. The cortex consists of five lobes, which have all kinds of mainly co-ordinating tasks.

Cingulate cortex – This area of the brain is involved in the perception of emotional and cognitive conflict.

Cyberball game – Computer ball game used to study the effects of exclusion.

Cytokines – These are proteins that send signals via the nervous system with regard to stimulating or moderating inflammation.

Default mode network (DMN) – The brain network that is active when there is no task to be conducted. Involved in autobiographical memory, thinking about the future, empathy and moral decision-making.

Differential susceptibility (DS) – This is a theory of Jay Belsky that describes that children who suffer substantially from negative environments also benefit substantially from positive situations.

Dopamine – A neurotransmitter that plays a role in attention, reward and motivation.

Dorsolateral prefrontal cortex (DLPFC) – This area in the prefrontal cortex controls higher-order cognitive processes: the more difficult rational tasks such as decision-making, complex tasks, and executive functions.

DRD4 – This polymorphic gene codes for the dopamine receptor D4. People with the 7-repeat variant have a less efficient dopamine receptor and an increased environmental sensitivity.

Emotional granularity (emotional literacy) – This means having many emotion words at your disposal. The more emotion words, the better your body can adapt.

Empathy – The ability to empathize with the other. Affective empathy: feeling the other person's emotion. Cognitive empathy: being able to put yourself in the other person's perspective.

Environmental sensitivity – This is a term from Michael Pluess that describes that some children are burdened by/benefit from their environment and others do not. Pluess uses this term as a synonym for biological sensitivity to context, differential susceptibility and sensory-processing sensitivity.

Fear of failure – The strong desire to prevent mistakes, through avoidance or through perfectionism. Fear of failure can be an effect of high sensitivity.

Frontal lobe – This is a part of the cerebral cortex involved in planning, memory, cognitive control, and decision making.

Habituation – The body learns that it does not have to respond to the stimulus present due to sensory adaptation. This is the opposite of sensitization.

Hippocampus – This is involved in memory: storing and retrieving experiences.

HPA axis – This is the abbreviation of the hypothalamus – pituitary – adrenal axis. This stimulates, among other things, the production of the stress hormone cortisol.

HSP – This is the abbreviation for highly sensitive person.

Hypothalamus – This regulates hunger, thirst, aggression, body temperature and sexual urges. It is also an important part of the stress system. The hypothalamus is involved in, among other things, the production of cortisol and (nor)adrenaline.

Inferior frontal gyrus (IFG) – This is an area of the brain that contains many mirror neurons. It is involved in the empathy.

Inhibited – With this term, Kagan described children who are reticent in new situations.

Insula – This is a part of the cerebral cortex that specializes in monitoring bodily sensations in conjunction with emotional and empathic processes. It plays a central role in interoception.

International Affective Picture System (IAPS) – This is a set of pictures that evoke (positive, negative or neutral) emotions.

Interoception – This is a sense that detects signals from the body (such as hunger, thirst and heart rate). It signals where there are shortages or surpluses. The insula plays a central role in this.

Latent Inhibition – This is the ability to exclude stimuli that seem irrelevant. Having a low latent inhibition means having difficulty locking out stimuli, but also appears to be related to creativity.

Limbic System – This consists of the hypothalamus, hippocampus, amygdala, and cingulate cortex.

Medial prefrontal cortex (mPFC) – This area in the prefrontal cortex is part of the social brain. It is active in judging others, judging yourself in relation to others, but also in empathizing with others.

Mentalizing (theory of mind) – This means being able to place yourself in the other's perspective. This requires understanding of the other's intentions.

Mirror neurons – These are neurons that respond to your own actions and the observed actions of others. These play a big part in empathy.

Neurons (nerve cells) – These are cells that specialize in receiving, processing, and transmitting information to and from other cells in the body. They are the basic building blocks of the brain.

Neurotransmitter – This is a substance that allows neurons to communicate with each other in the synapse. A synapse is the space between two neurons in which neurotransmitters transfer from one neuron to another. Some examples of neurotransmitters: adrenaline, norepinephrine, serotonin and oxytocin.

Occipital lobe – This is a part of the cerebral cortex that processes visual information.

Orbitofrontal Cortex (OFC) – This is a part of the frontal lobe involved in the assessment of rewards.

Overstimulation – Overstimulation occurs when there is an imbalance between the incoming stimuli and the ability to process them. When the brain can no longer handle the amount of stimuli, it intervenes. Overstimulation can be an effect of the high sensitivity trait, but it is not an inseparable part of it.

Oxytocin – This is a hormone and neurotransmitter that, in short, is involved in attachment. The oxytocin receptor OXTR regulates the ability to absorb this hormone and has three variants: AA, AG and GG.

Parietal Lobe – This is part of the cerebral cortex. This area regulates and senses all motor and sensory activity in the body.

Polymorphism – This means that there are different manifestations of something. When it comes to DNA it means that there are different variations of genes.

Prediction Cycle – This is the description of how the brain works, according to Lisa Feldman Barrett. The brain predicts, simulates, compares and corrects errors.

Salience network (SN) – This brain network consists of areas of the brain that are mainly activated by striking events in the environment and ensures that attention remains focused on them. To this end, it suppresses activity in the DMN.

Sally-Anne test – This is a neuropsychological experiment to test the ability to empathize with the other.

SAM (Sympathetic-Adrenal Medullary System) – It is a rapid connection between hypothalamus, adrenal medullary and autonomic nervous system that stimulates the production of stress hormones ((nor)adrenaline).

Self-compassion – This is the ability to treat yourself with care and attention when faced with personal failure or painful life situations.

Sensitization – This is the phenomenon that occurs when neurons become more sensitive. In this case, offering a stimulus more often leads to an enhanced response. Sensitization is the opposite of habituation.

Sensory adaptation – Receptor cells become less sensitive when a stimulus is presented at the same level for a certain time. You perceive the sensations less.

Sensory-processing sensitivity (SPS) – This is the scientific name for the high sensitivity trait.

Serotonin – This is a neurotransmitter that affects memory, confidence, sleep, emotions, sexual activity, appetite, cognition (such as learning, attention, planning) and social behavior. It also plays a role in the processing of pain stimuli.

Stress – Stress consists of any stimulus that activates the SAM system (with the associated release of adrenaline and norepinephrine) and the HPA axis (thereby producing ACTH and cortisol).

Temporal Lobe – This is a part of the cerebral cortex that processes auditory information.

Temporo-parietal junction (TPJ) – This is an area of the brain between the temporal and parietal lobe that is important in mentalizing. It is therefore linked to cognitive empathy.

Thalamus – This area of the brain receives all sensory information and sends it to areas in the cerebral cortex for further processing. It is part of the brain stem. Together with the hypothalamus, it forms the intermediate brain.

Theory of mind (mentalizing) – Being able to put yourself in the perspective of the other. This requires understanding of the intentions of the other.

Trier Social Stress Test (TSST) – This test examines people's stress response when they are judged by a distant jury after having had very little preparation time.

Uninhibited – This is the term Kagan used to describe children who approach situations easily.

Vantage sensitivity – This is Michael Pluess' theory that describes how some people benefit greatly from positive circumstances.

Ventral striatum – This is part of the basal ganglia. Here, the emotional value of an action is determined.

Ventral tegmental area (VTA) – This area is part of the basal ganglia that aims to register whether an event is rewarding or disappointing.

Wisconsin card sorting test (WCST) – This is a test to detect cognitive flexibility disorders.

5-HTTLPR – The polymorphic gene 5-HTTLPR plays a role in serotonin transport. There are three variations: s/s, s/l and l/l. The s/s variant is associated with high sensitivity.

Acknowledgements

My first word of thanks goes to Elaine Aron. My own process of exploring, recognizing and acknowledging high sensitivity started with her books. I had the opportunity to personally thank her for this, but I also want to do it here. Pioneers like her are extremely important. They stick their necks out. To spread knowledge that is sometimes viewed with suspicion, but is so supportive for those who identify with it. During her seminars, Elaine Aron radiates that, first and foremost, she simply is a highly sensitive person, but the knowledge she shares is incredibly thorough and comprehensive.

Her approach inspired me to conduct my own research. Secondly, I would like to thank the many thousands of people who took part in my studies, anywhere in the world. Your openness provides a much better idea of what high sensitivity actually means. Your experiences color the theories. In my opinion, the combination of both is essential. Insights from science provide a solid framework for understanding daily experiences. As a result, we have been able to discover connections that would otherwise remain hidden from view. Researchers who, in addition to Elaine Aron, have strongly inspired me are Lisa Feldman Barrett, Brené Brown and Bianca Acevedo.

I am very grateful to my colleagues from all over the world. In the first place Karina Zegers de Beijl for supporting my (research) work in many ways. Thanks also to Prof. Judith Homberg, professor at the Donders Institute for Brain, Cognition and Behavior, for her reaction and additions to a previous edition. Any inaccuracies are, of course, at my expense. For the opportunity to be able to inspire people beyond the borders of the Netherlands, I would like to thank Vertaalbureau Textwerk B.V., Julie Bjelland, Maria Hill, April Snow, Rosie Raleigh, Nicole Burgess, Lian Kirksæther, Patricia Young & Fiona Stevenson. In addition, thanks to publisher Suzanna van der Laan of Booklight, who mobilized a team of professionals to realize this beautiful copy.

Writing a book is an intensive process that also affects close family and friends. My apologies to all of you for my regular absence and thank you for your patience and encouragement. I would like to mention one person in particular: my partner Derk, who not only encouraged me, but also relieved me and created the supportive environment which made it possible to write this book. For a highly sensitive woman like me, you truly are a gift!

About the author

Drs. Esther Bergsma is an expert on high sensitivity. With her (international) research as a social science researcher, she has given high sensitivity a scientific and human face.
Esther studied Public Administration at the University of Twente, specializing in methods and techniques of social science research. She worked as a (coordinating) researcher and manager within the Ministry of Social Affairs and Employment and, before her burnout, was a manager at a service organization. After her burnout, she started her own practice specializing in high sensitivity.

Her first book, *Hoogsensitieve kinderen* (Highly Sensitive Children), is popular among parents and professionals. In the foreword of the book, Elaine Aron praises the practical applicability of the book and the new research directions offered.

Esther trains professionals to better understand and guide highly sensitive people. She educates doctors and psychologists regarding the scientific background of the trait and speaks in-depth with HSP coaches. She is also a frequent speaker at conferences and study days.

She founded the platform Hoogsensitief.NL enabling more and more people to explore, recognize and acknowledge the high sensitivity trait. The website contains hundreds of blogs from different authors on various aspects of high sensitivity, including some English blogs. Bergsma also published results from her studies there. With her book The Brain of the Highly Sensitive Person, she hopes that highly sensitive talent will be recognized and acknowledged more quickly, so that both HSPs and society can flourish.